JAPAN
— from —
A to Z

JAPAN
from
A *to* Z

MYSTERIES OF EVERYDAY LIFE
EXPLAINED

James M. Vardaman, Jr.
Michiko Sasaki Vardaman

YENBOOKS

We dedicate this book to our daughter
Maya
with the hope that she will share our curiosity
about how people do things, and why

Illustrated by Yuko Munakata

YENBOOKS
2-6, Suido 1-chome, Bunkyo-ku, Tokyo 112, Japan

LCC Card No. 95-61407
ISBN 4-900737-41-0

First edition, 1995

Printed in Japan

Acknowledgments

We would like to thank the following people for their encouragement and willingness to share their knowledge, but more than anything for their curiosity: Roger Finch, Martin Foulds, Lewis Hargan, Toyotomi Morimoto, Fumiteru Nitta, Kotaro Oizumi, Mizuho Sawada, Yasuo Uchida, David Vardaman, Linda Vardaman, Maya Vardaman, and Mizue Yoshino.

We owe a special word of thanks to our editor David Friedman, who devoted himself to this project as if it were his own. This book would be far less accurate and readable without his incisive comments and sure editorial hand.

Introduction

Have you ever gotten caught short of cash late at night and wondered why Japanese banks don't dispense cash twenty-four hours a day? Have you ever been surprised by a Japanese friend's breaking his or her wooden chopsticks at the end of a meal? Has it ever occurred to you that you've never seen a woman sushi chef.

Japan, like any other country, abounds with customs that will appear to many foreigners as quaint, humorous, surprising, or occasionally even troublesome. Above all, non-Japanese—and sometimes even Japanese themselves—may find some aspects of life in Japan incomprehensible. The fact is, though, that Japanese culture and customs have not evolved at random. They all have their origins in the actions and beliefs of people from days gone by, whether in the distant past, or in more recent times.

This book seeks to answer questions that people, from tourists to long-term residents, might have about the country that's given the world karaoke, sushi, and cheap VCRs. For the most part, the topics it discusses are not issues of earth-shattering importance. Rather, they are ones that arise during the course of daily life and/or travel. We chose topics like this by design; our hope was to identify and address questions whose answers might not be readily apparent but could become available to anyone who was curious enough simply to ask questions. Where several answers were equally plausible, we have noted that fact, but generally we have chosen the reply that seems best documented and most authoritative on the basis of our own research.

In many cases it's not even the questions that make the items appealing, but the answers. For instance, many people may never even have noticed how hirsute the men on Japanese paper money are, let alone wondered why. But the reason why they do so is actually rather interesting (See the entry on "CURRENCY").

We hope you'll find this book informative and, at the same time, fun. Beyond that, we hope it will encourage you to ask more questions about your surroundings. Perhaps the single greatest life-enriching word is the short and simple "why."

JAPAN
—from—
A to Z

Why is AKIHABARA the center of Tokyo's electrical appliance market?

As a result of the incendiary bombings of World War II, only a narrow strip of buildings was left between the Kanda and Akihabara districts by the time hostilities had ended. This area became a gathering point for black marketeers hawking foodstuffs, clothing, and a few electrical items such as light bulbs, vacuum tubes, and radio parts. The black market was suppressed in 1949, but the radio parts dealers gathered under the train overpass near Akihabara, right by the main train lines, and continued selling items that flowed out of U.S. Army bases. The wholesalers came along with the black-and-white television boom, and Akihabara quickly became the place to buy electrical goods of all kinds.

What are those grinning ANIMALS in front of drinkeries?

The happily mischievous-looking characters in front of many *izakaya*, or Japanese-style taverns, are called *tanuki*. In Japanese folklore, the *tanuki*, a badger-like animal, has long been considered an amusing and shrewd animal with supernatural powers. Able to transform himself into a beautiful maiden or an old woman in a flash, the *tanuki* is not to be trusted, but at the same time his whimsical character has endeared him to Japanese for centuries. A large statue of a standing *tanuki* with an umbrella hat, a large belly, enormous testicles, and a bottle of saké in one hand can often be found in front of an *izakaya*, perhaps as advertisement of the magical products being sold within.

Why are APPLES *always peeled before being eaten*?

In the days when a main source of fertilizer was night soil, it was wise not to eat the skin of fruit; but this fact also applies to the agricultural chemicals that are used in contemporary times to produce virtually unblemished fruit.

Why do some cars in Japan have green-and-yellow, ARROW-shaped marks?

These two-toned *wakaba māku*, or "young leaf," symbols are required by law when a driver is newly licensed. New drivers must affix them to their cars for the first year after receiving their licenses, so that other motorists can make allowances for their lack of driving experience. It is an offense to unnecessarily hassle such drivers, however poor or annoying their driving habits may be. Even if drivers are not newly licensed, there is in fact no penalty for affixing these magnetic symbols to their cars even after the one-year mandatory period if they feel they need special

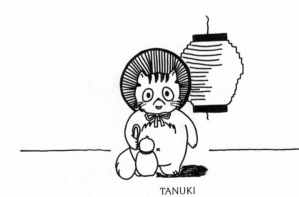

TANUKI

consideration because of their lack of skill at the wheel.

Why don't AUTOMATIC TELLER MACHINES operate twenty-four hours a day?

There are three main reasons that banks do not make their ATMs available all night and all day. First, they feel they need time to shut the machines down for maintenance. Next, if the machines were to be up around the clock, it would become necessary to hire security personnel to watch over them. Finally, they simply don't detect a demand for round-the-clock cashing services and feel that extending banking hours would be a money-losing proposition.

Which nation sells the most AUTOMOBILES to Japan?

Figures for 1993 show that Germany is far and away the winner in this category. The top selling imported cars in that year were manufactured by Mercedes Benz (top), BMW (third), Volkswagen (fourth), and Opel (fifth). Second place was held by an American firm—Honda U.S.A.

RANDOSERU

What are black and red leather BACKPACKS for?

These packs are on prominent display in department stores in February and March, in anticipation of the start of school in April. Called *randoseru*, from the Dutch word *ransel*, these bags are for elementary school students to carry their textbooks and stationery in. They are used for school only and are not carried for traveling or going to "cram" schools. The original model was a military knapsack, and *randoseru* first appeared in 1885 when the students of Gakushuin, a school for the children of the aristocracy, began carrying them to school. They became popular among children of the upper class in Tokyo, then became popular nationwide after World War II. The colors black, for boys, and red, for girls, have been conservatively maintained. Unusual colors like pink or blue seem to invite teasing from classmates.

When do Japanese say BANZAI?

The very first use of *banzai* appears in records of Emperor Kanmu's transfer of the capital to Heiankyo (now Kyoto). Of Chinese origin, this word meaning "long life" was at first used to express respect for the Emperor. Originally the word was not *banzai*, but *banzei*. It is written with the characters for "ten thousand" and "years-old."

Raising both hands and cheering *banzai* first became customary in 1889 upon the promulgation of the Meiji Constitution. The idea was promoted as a way of celebrating the new laws of the land. At present, the custom of raising one's arms in the air and shouting *banzai* three times has come to be a way of giving three cheers for a person or achievement.

When did BASEBALL first come to Japan? When was the first team established?

The first baseball game played in Japan was in 1873 at the forerunner of the modern-day University of Tokyo. The sport gradually grew popular and was played in middle schools from the turn of the century. The first professional team was established in 1934, and the present professional league made its debut in 1950.

Why do American BASEBALL players come to Japan to play?

With several major exceptions, players with American major league experience sign on with Japanese teams either very early or very late in their careers. Japanese professional teams have a mutual agreement to play no more than two non-Japanese players during regular season games, but those two players may have just the right talents to spur the team on to victory. A player at the end of a major league career may have the experience and sufficient strength to play at least on a par with most Japanese players, and the financial rewards for a big hitter are significant.

Why do high school BASEBALL players take home dirt from Koshien Stadium?

If a broadcast continues long enough, you will see players gathering dirt from the field of this arena in Osaka at the end of every game of the twice-annual high school baseball tournament. Soil has special meaning to many Japanese, who feel that earth from sacred areas has protective power. For high school baseball players, Koshien is a sacred place, and the soil symbolizes their sweat and tears. The teams collect soil to scatter on their home fields as an inspiration to work hard and return to the next tournament. It also makes a nice bit of memorabilia.

Why do the Japanese throw BEANS at demons in February?

A custom that originated in China, the expulsion of "demons" such as epidemics and calamities was originally carried out in the imperial court on the last day of the year to prepare for a new year of good fortune. Before long, the custom spread to the general populace and came to be practiced at the most important of the four divisions of the year, the one at the beginning of spring when the agricultural year began. For the farmers who made up the core of Japan's agrarian society, the act of expelling demons expressed hopes for good weather and good harvests. Today the custom is continued by families who open all the doors and windows of their homes and throw beans outside while saying *Oni wa soto, fuku wa uchi*, or "Demons out, good fortune in." Walk through any Japanese neighborhood the morning after *mame-maki*, or "bean throwing," and the beans along the street will show just how many people observe this tradition.

Why are beans the anti-demon missile of choice? Because *mame*, or "bean," can also mean "evil eye" or "evil diminishing," when written with different characters.

Who uses BEEPERS?

One expects business people to carry *poke-beru* (from "pocket bell"), as they are called in Japanese, but the popularity of these status goods goes way beyond the world of work. As of February 1995, it was estimated that there were over 9.3 million beepers in use in Japan, and that a significant portion of these were used by female high school students.

For what could they possibly use these *poke-beru*, which until recently have only been capable of displaying numbers? To aid in this form of communication, a Tokyo publisher put out a list of special beeper codes, selling two hundred thousand copies in two months in 1994. The book uses alternate readings of Japanese numbers to include over three hundred fifty messages that vary from a simple "good morning" (0840 = O-*ha-yo-o*) or "good night" (0833731 = O-*ya-su-mi-na-sa-i*), to "I'll wait for you at the west exit of Shinjuku Station." (02-40109-240 = Ma-*tsu shi-n-ju-ku ni-shi-guchi*)

The popularity of these beepers appears to be due to the perennial desire to belong to the group. What else would account for learning three hundred fifty codes for anything?

Why are Japanese BEER bottles the same size and shape?

Beer brewers Asahi and Sapporo were once part of the same company, and for many years they shared bottles as an economic convenience. In 1963, Suntory joined them in an agreement to purchase bottles that all three brewers could recycle with their own labels. A close look at the 633-milliliter bottles will tell you that, despite the great variety of labels, caps, and contents, only the word "beer" is actually engraved on these companies' bottles. Competitor Kirin, which has traditionally maintained the largest market share within Japan, uses softer-shouldered bottles with its name on them.

Why do some Japanese wear BELLY BANDS?

Japanese people have long felt it important to keep the stomach warm in order to keep healthy, because they regard the stomach as the body's center. Several decades ago, one often saw men in the heat of summer with only T-shirts for tops but wearing stomach warmers made of stretchable wool material over them.

Why do Japanese put BIBS on some Buddhist statues?

One of the most popular of the bodhisattvas of Buddhism in Japan is known as Jizo. Usually he is represented with a jewel in one hand and a staff in the other. Because of his vow to aid all suffering beings, he became regarded especially as the savior of children, and statues of Jizo along roadsides are often decorated with bibs provided by worshippers.

What is the most common form of BIRTH CONTROL in Japan?

Condoms account for 80% of birth control in Japan and have a long and venerable history as an important part of Japan's sex life. As far back as the Pacific War, even the Japanese troops who abused comfort

JIZO

women were required to use condoms by commanders terrified that their troops' combat effectiveness would be impaired by venereal disease. In contemporary Japan's prostitution industry, as well, condom use is prevalent, especially in this age of AIDS.

Why did the BIRTHRATE drop in 1966?

Due to a superstition that women born in the forty-third year, or *hinoe uma*, of the traditional sixty-year cycle had an unmanageable disposition, there was usually a drop in the birth rate during that year of each cycle. The last year this occurred was 1966, and, sure enough, the number of births dropped that year.

Why do Japanese men wear BLACK both to weddings and funerals?

Black is the color for formal events, and men may wear the same suit both to weddings and funerals, but the color of the necktie will differ. At weddings men wear white ties, while at funerals they wear black ones. Traditionally, women wedding guests who are married wear kimono with black backgrounds overlaid with gold, silver, or multicolored patterning. Plain, black, silk kimono with no design are appropriate for funerals. The dark, sober clothing prevents guests from upstaging the elaborately dressed bride and groom.

Why is the BON festival celebrated at two different times?

Japanese Buddhist tradition holds that the spirits of the ancestors return to visit their families between the thirteenth and fifteenth days of the seventh month of the year. On the Gregorian calendar, of course, the seventh month is July, but if one goes in accordance with the old lunar calendar observed by Japanese farmers, the seventh month corresponds with our August. As a result, some localities observe the event in mid-July, while others observe it in mid-August. Recently, some companies have been giving their employees mid-August vacations to coincide with school summer holidays, rather than encouraging observance of the holiday in July.

What is in all those little BOTTLES that people buy at kiosks and drugstores?

So-called health drinks often come in bottles made of brown glass and range from ¥120 for Vitamin C mixed with caffeine, to much more princely sums for royal jelly, ginseng root, or tincture of snake (parts of a snake in solution).

Why are plastic BOTTLES filled with water and set up against walls, telephone poles, and flower beds?

Some people insist that the reflections from the water bottles are disturbing to area alley cats, who see their faces distorted as they walk by. As a result, these nuisances will stay away, and avoid doing their business on people's property. This practice seems to have no practical effect, but people continue to do so nonetheless.

NHK reports that the rumor of the bottles' effectiveness may have come from Australia as early as 1987, but the rapid spread of the bottles in the spring and summer of 1994 apparently resulted from the fact that one of the groundskeepers at Tokyo Electric put bottles all around a certain facility. Local residents who witnessed the practice became convinced that it must offer some benefit. The cat-repelling bottles made the national news when a bottle filled with water caused a fire by focusing sunlight on discarded lumber. Now *that* would scare a cat away.

When meeting someone on business, how and when should you BOW?

At the very outset, one makes a perfunctory bow, which carries you through until you know who the person is. Only after exchanging business cards and determining the status relationship between you and the other person do you make the formal bow at an appropriate angle, along with the accompanying greeting. However democratic one might wish to be, it is a faux pas to bow equally low to the president of a company and a clerk. It is awkward for the other person when you over- or underdo a bow.

When were the first "station BOX LUNCHES" introduced?

E*ki-ben* is a shortened amalgamation of *eki*, or "station," and *bentō*, or "box lunch." In its very first incarnation, the *eki-ben* was a rather spartan affair first sold at Utsunomiya Station in 1885. It consisted simply of

TSUNO-KAKUSHI

two rice balls with pickled plum inside, all wrapped up in a bamboo leaf. The *maku-no-uchi* type of box lunch which is common today dates from 1888 and was first sold at Himeji Station in the Kansai area. It consisted of white rice, fried egg, boiled fish paste, fried fish, and pickled daikon.

What are those knobbed metal BRACELETS that some Japanese men wear?

These bracelets are originally from Spain, where they are believed to effectively reduce tension. In Japan they sell for around ¥20,000 and have enjoyed a boom among golfers who believe that it helps with putting. Even after the burst of the bubble and consequent plunge in sales of golf clubs, these bracelets, sold in the golf equipment section, have continued to sell well. Some purchasers claim that the bracelets have even lowered their blood pressure, but stores are careful to refer to them merely as fashion accessories.

How do Japanese make black BREAD?

Researchers in Aomori Prefecture have found that the ink of squid has certain anti-cancer properties, and this scholarship has found its way to an unlikely group of beneficiaries: bakers in search of a new product. As a result, ink-black French bread has appeared at the forefront of the squid-ink cuisine boom of 1993. Black butter anyone?

Why do BRIDES wear a white head dressing?

This part of the traditional wedding attire is called *tsuno-kakushi*, or "horn hider." Japanese have traditionally believed that a woman might grow mad from jealousy, sprout horns, and turn into a demon; this head dressing was originally a talisman to prevent such a thing from occurring.

Why do BRIDES *change clothing during the wedding reception?*

Iro-naoshi, literally "color changing," when the bride is escorted out of the hall to change clothes and then reenters, occurs at least once, and often several times during the wedding reception.

The origins of the custom date from the Nara period, when the new bride wore white for the first three days after marriage, then on the fourth day changed into clothing dyed in the color of her husband's household. At the beginning of the modern era the bride wore attire with the crest of her own family to the ceremony and there changed into clothing with the crest of her husband's family. Today's multiple changes, in which even the groom may change clothes, is little more than a pageant with little to do with tradition.

Why is the BUDDHA *depicted the way he is?*

The Buddha is depicted in so many scrolls and statues in Japan that one tends to forget that for almost five centuries after his death no one—even in his homeland—sculpted or painted likenesses of him. It was only in the first century A.D. that images of the founder of Buddhism came to be produced. These depictions, which would set the tone for virtually all images of the Buddha thereafter, reflected the Indian view of the characteristics of superior human beings. An "excellent" being was held to have large feet, a tiny curl of white hair in the center of the forehead, and specially curled hair.

Where is the biggest statue of the BUDDHA in Japan?

Completed in 752, the 15-meter-tall Daibutsu (literally, "big Buddha") at Todaiji Temple in Nara could hold seventeen smallish people in its left hand. It is enclosed in what is believed to be the largest wooden edifice in existence. The construction of Todaiji, its outer buildings, and the statues it houses are said to have required the labor of over 2 million workers.

Why do Japanese pour sweet tea on statues of the BUDDHA?

On April 8, the birthday of the Buddha, worshippers sprinkle a figure of the infant Buddha with sweet tea, or *ama-cha*, as a rite of bathing the Buddha called *kanbutsue*. The tea is symbolic of the scented water which nine dragons are said to have poured over the infant when he was born.

Are Japanese BUDDHISTS or Shintoists?

According to the "Religion Yearbook" issued by the Agency for Cultural Affairs, most Japanese are a little of both. The data supplied by various religious organizations indicates that the number of members in Shinto-related groups is close to 120 million, and that of Buddhist groups is close to 90 million. Add Christian and various other organizations, and the total becomes 220 million members—about twice the population of Japan. This apparent contradiction can be explained easily. Japanese tend to follow Shinto observances for celebratory and auspicious events and Buddhist observances for inauspicious events such as funerals and memorials. They share neither the monotheistic, nor the one-religion-per-customer proclivities of Westerners.

What is the meaning of the figurines of a CAT with its paw raised?

Often made of pottery or papier-mâché, these *maneki-neko*, or "beckoning cats," are displayed in front of eating and drinking establishments. They appear to be using the Japanese gesture for beckoning and are posed so as to invite customers into their masters' shops.

Traditionally, a *maneki-neko's* left paw was raised above its ear, and sometimes the right paw held a small gold coin. One possible source for the origin of this figure is a ninth-century Chinese work which says that when a cat washes its face even to the point of cleaning behind its ear, a guest is going to appear.

A more recent Japanese story tells of a fishmonger who became ill and unable to work and subsequently fell into dire straits. A stray cat whom he had be-friended and to whom he had often given leftovers appeared on his doorstep bearing a gold coin in its mouth, thus momentarily solving his financial needs.

Even a brief look at the *maneki-neko* in restaurant and tavern windows will reveal that not all have their left paws raised. The modern understanding of this is that the right paw beckons "good fortune," and the

MANEKI-NEKO

left paw beckons "customers." From the point of view of the shop, of course, the end result is the same.

What is the connection between CATFISH and earthquakes?

Long ago, people thought that earthquakes were caused by the shaking of a giant catfish living underground. When the catfish would stir, either from restlessness, or its displeasure at human folly, it would send the surface of the earth into convulsions. Since the late Edo period (1600-1868), catfish have been thought capable of predicting earthquakes by showing increased movement just prior to an occurrence.

Why is it that girls CELEBRATE their third and seventh years, but boys only celebrate their fifth year?

At three, kids were allowed to let their hair grow out, and at five boys were allowed to wear *hakama* for the first time. Eventually, this custom developed into celebrating the boys' fifth year by dressing them in kimono with *hakama*. At seven girls began to tie real *obi* to wear with their kimono.

What kinds of meats are called "CHERRY blossom" and "peony" in Japanese?

Botan, or "peony," is a euphemism for the meat of wild boar, especially when cooked with vegetables and tofu in a pot with miso flavoring. *Sakura*, or "cherry blossom," is horse meat.

Why are carp banners flown on CHILDREN'S DAY?

Carp have a good image in Japan—witness the name of Hiroshima's professional baseball team. Since carp can swim upstream against strong currents, they have

KOI-NOBORI

become symbols of stamina and courage. That is why you can see huge carp banners, or *koi-nobori*, vigorously "swimming" in the spring breeze during the weeks around May 5. The top banner is multicolored, followed by a black carp symbolizing the father, a red carp symbolizing the mother, and other carp—usually blue—for each of the boys (and sometimes girls, too) in the family.

What's wrong with sticking CHOPSTICKS upright into a bowl of rice?

It is Buddhist custom to make occasional offerings of rice to the deceased. One offers rice by putting a bowl of it on the family altar and sticking a pair of chopsticks into it, pointing straight up. Thus, sticking chopsticks into one's rice at mealtime makes the food look like a death-offering and is considered inauspicious. It should be noted, though, that many young Japanese are blissfully ignorant of this belief and do not always observe the custom.

Why do Japanese break their disposable CHOPSTICKS after use?

Japanese do not always do this, but it happens often enough to make one wonder why. The source of this custom seems to be that it was once believed that if one did not break one's chopsticks after eating a meal in a field or mountain, some evil spirit would attach itself to the used chopsticks and cause the eater to fall ill. Disposable chopsticks, or *waribashi*, have therefore come to be regarded as single-use utensils that are to be used by no one else; breaking them prevents reuse from occurring even by chance. Even in the home, there is still a tendency for each member of the family to have his or her own pair and not to share chopsticks.

On a related note, this tradition of not reusing chopsticks also helps explain why wooden chopsticks are stuck together, rather than split apart, before use. Machine-cut, wooden *waribashi* are left attached at one end to indicate that they have not been used by another. They are split apart on use and then disposed of. The recycling movement may one day affect this custom.

What percentage of Japanese who celebrate Christmas are CHRISTIAN?

Despite the popularity of Christmas "decoration cakes," and the fact that many young couples go to romantic restaurants for dinner on Christmas Eve, few Japanese are actually Christian. The Christian-style wedding so popular among Japanese, for example, often takes place in a "chapel" within a hotel or wedding hall where the brief ceremony is part of a package which includes photographs, reception, and gifts. The "minister," who may never meet the couple until the ceremony, has no legal status during the proceedings, as the formal registration of the marriage is done by the couple themselves at the local ward or city office. The membership of Christian churches was estimated at 0.7% of Japan's population by the Agency of Cultural Affairs in 1993.

Why is COFFEE sometimes served with special brown sugar?

This "coffee sugar" is made of caramel added to granulated sugar which is recrystallized and then cracked. It gives the savory fragrance of sweet caramel and strongly brings out the aroma of the coffee.

Why is a cup of COFFEE so expensive in Japan?

It is not that the coffee is imported or that an excessive duty has been levied on the beans that warrants coffee prices of ¥400 and up at coffee shops. Rather, the charge is better seen as rent: for a very reasonable price, one can sit and recuperate, undisturbed, from the crowds when out shopping, or just sit and read for hours on end, while the waiter or waitress pleasantly refills your glass with water.

Why do ¥5 and ¥50 COINS have holes?

When the Japanese economy was based on the *sen* (¥0.01) rather than the yen, there were several coins with circular holes in the middle. During the first half of this century the holes disappeared and coins were distinguished by size and material. There was also a time when there were not so many denominations of coins, so one of two distinctions sufficed. Today, however, we have coins of ¥1, ¥5, ¥10, ¥50, ¥100, and ¥500 value. Size alone, even with the addition of tooled edges, is insufficient to help the user recognize the denomination. The hole was, therefore, reintroduced to help even people with limited sight distinguish between ¥5 and ¥10 coins and ¥50 and ¥100 coins by feel alone.

Why do so many high school graduates go on to COLLEGE?

According to a 1993 survey carried out by the Ministry of Education, 40.9% of high school grads went on to some form of continued education.

A look at the difference between the average first month's pay for new employees helps to explain the desire to spend four more years in school. In 1992, the average monthly pay for male college grads was ¥186,000, while female college grads earned ¥180,000. By comparison, male high school graduates earned ¥146,000 as an average starting salary, and their female counterparts made ¥139,000.

Despite the steady advance of salaries in proportion to the length of time people spend in their jobs, the college graduate's wage catches up with that of the person whose education ended with high school, despite the latter's head start on joining the work force.

How long is the average worker's COMMUTE?

A 1990 national survey carried out by the Management and Coordination Agency reports that the average commute (one way) takes between one and one and a half hours for 40% of commuters to workplaces in urban Tokyo, Nagoya, and Osaka. At the same time, for each of the past several years, numbers of commuter passes issued for the *shinkansen* lines have risen 30% to 50% over the previous year. Thus, while commuting time may not be rising, distances are still growing.

What can you do with a "COMPANION"?

At virtually any large stand-up buffet sponsored by large enterprises or business associations, there is a squad of attractive ladies, not always young, who assist the attendees with finding food and drink. They also serve as conversation partners. Often engaged for the duration of the party, they are only intended to add a feminine touch to the proceedings and are in no way available for further entertainment purposes.

Why are bamboo and streamers attached to ridgepoles of houses during CONSTRUCTION?

When carpenters have completed the framework of a house, they attach bamboo poles with multicolored streamers called *gohei* (similar to the ones at shrines) to the ridgepole. This practice is intended to invoke divine protection in protecting the builders from misfortune during the remaining construction. There may also be a ceremonial bow and arrow secured to the top of the framework positioned to "shoot down" any potential misfortune that is likely to come from the northeast, considered an inauspicious direction. When constructing a house, the builders usually carry out a ceremony in which the carpenters throw rice cakes from the roof to the crowd below and a small party on the property, where the owner feasts the builders.

Why are dead bodies CREMATED and not buried?

Archaeologists tell us that during the Jomon and Yayoi periods, the Japanese practiced burial customs similar to those of the West today. That is, bodies were placed in jars or coffins and buried in the ground. This custom began to change after the introduction of Buddhism, which held that the body should be cremated so that its soul could be reborn. Because the imperial family and members of the court were the first to adopt Buddhism, it was among the elite that the custom of cremation first took hold; but with the popularization of Buddhism commencing in the twelfth century, the practice spread to the common people. Cremation remains the almost universal form of corpse disposal in Japan.

Why are the men on Japanese CURRENCY so hairy?

This is not only due to the fact that men in earlier ages wore more facial hair. One of the prerequisites for appearing on the bills is to offer opportunities for lots of detail—whether in the form of a beard, a mustache, or wrinkles—to prevent counterfeiting. Writer Higuchi Ichiyo was a candidate in the last selection of people, but she was eliminated from competition not because of her sex, but because she was too much of a beauty.

How did CURRY make its way to Japan?

Curry powder was introduced to Japan in the late Edo period by the English. During the late Meiji period (1868–1912), the Japanese version of curry roux was developed and the dish called *karē raisu* was born. The dish has been popular since the 1920s and ranks among the favorite "Japanese dishes" of people of every age group.

What happened to the arms and legs of DARUMA dolls?

Daruma dolls represent the Indian priest Bodhidharma, who founded Chinese Zen Buddhism and is said to have lost the use of his appendages as a result of

DARUMA

spending nine years in seated meditation. In Japan, where his name has been transformed into Daruma, his single-mindedness toward achieving a goal has made him an ideal symbol for the fulfillment of a particular wish. Papier-mâché *daruma* are made so that they will right themselves whenever they are tipped over, symbolic of not surrendering to despair when times are tough.

Why do **DARUMA** *dolls have no eyes?*

Approximately 80% of the *daruma* of Japan are produced in Gunma Prefecture in the city of Takasaki. In 1783, nearby volcano Mt. Azuma exploded in a tremendous eruption, leaving the surrounding area barren and suffering from famine. The abbot of a local temple made wooden models of a painting of Bodhidharma and helped poor farmers there make papier-mâché dolls as a means of earning a living.

These daruma do not have eyes for several reasons. First, Bodhidharma did not use the visible eye to achieve enlightenment but the eye of the mind. Second, an image of the Buddha is said to come to life only when the eye is painted in. Finally, there is a pun on the sound *gan*, which can mean either "request" or "eye," depending on the character used to write it.

Dolls depicting Daruma are most commonly used by candidates for political office. The candidate paints in one eye when his campaign begins and the other eye upon winning the election.

Which eye should you fill in first? Facing the *daruma*, paint in his left eye when you make your wish. Paint in the eye on the right when your wish is fulfilled, then take it to the local shrine or temple as an offering. *Daruma* and other felicitous ornaments are usually burned in a bonfire at New Year's.

Where did the Japanese names for the DAYS of the week come from?

It seems unclear who declared that Japan would adopt the Western calendar with its seven-day week, but the solar calendar was adopted in 1872. It is also unclear who decided that Sunday would be called *nichiyōbi* and so on, but the Japanese names of the other days do not follow the English names. Rather, they follow the continental western European model in associating the days with the heavenly spheres in this order: the Sun, the Moon, Mars, Mercury, Jupiter, Venus, and Saturn.

Whom do Japanese visit in order to talk to DEAD family members?

Mediums, who gather at Mt. Osore in Aomori Prefecture during the summer festival there, work at helping to establish communication with the other world.

Why do Japanese put out DECORATIONS made of bamboo and pine in front of their houses at New Year's?

The god of the New Year is welcomed at each house because he or she brings good crops, good business, or a good catch of fish, depending on the type of occupation in which the inhabitants of the house engage. The god needs a place to reside during the visit from January 1 through the seventh (in some places until the fifteenth), and the bamboo-and-pine *kado-matsu* provides those temporary quarters.

How did early DEPARTMENT stores tackle the Japanese custom of "no shoes indoors"?

Through the Meiji period, stores and shops did not, as a rule, put their goods on display. A customer would come and ask to see certain items, then sit in the open area near the entrance of the shop while the clerks went to the storeroom and brought out the merchandise. The Western idea of a department store, where goods are on display and the customer walks around freely, presented the daunting problem of

KADO-MATSU

how to deal with customers' footwear. Prior to the Great Kanto Earthquake of 1923, shops provided slippers for customers. This practice, however, often brought about confusion at the entranceway, where footwear was checked and later reclaimed. Even small shops were at a disadvantage because their clerks could only handle limited numbers of pairs of footwear.

Finally, not long after the giant earthquake, two big Nihonbashi stores launched a revolution—they let their customers keep their shoes on! As a result, there were no more bottlenecks at the entrance and no more need for clerks to run back and forth to the storerooms.

Why is the "one" spot on Japanese DICE red?

The passion for red began in the middle of this century, when a producer in Wakayama decided to make its product stand out from those of other Japanese producers. As is often the case, other manufacturers simply followed suit, and the red dot became the norm. Dots for the export market, though, are still made with all their dots a uniform black.

What is a "DOCTOR STOP"?

There are times when a physician may prevent an athlete from continuing participation in a competition, or forbid a patient to drink alcohol. This odd combination of English words refers to the advice or stronger admonition of a doctor to avoid a certain activity, food, or beverage. Japanese-language dictionaries list it as a term referring to stopping a boxing match on a doctor's orders, and this would appear to be the origin of the expression.

Who is the most famous DOG in Japan?

This honor undoubtedly goes to an Akita dog named Hachiko, who is commemorated with a statue in the plaza on the east side of the JR station at Shibuya. Legend tells that the dog would go to the station every evening to greet his master and escort him home. Even after his master's demise, Hachiko unfailingly went to the station each evening and waited for train after train, in the process becoming a famous figure. A year after Hachiko died on March 8, 1935, a statue was erected in honor of his loyalty. The current statue dates from after World War II and remains one of the best-known meeting places in Tokyo.

What is the connection between pregnant women and DOGS?

It is believed that dogs bear offspring without great difficulty, so "dog days" are considered auspicious days to visit shrines and purchase amulets for the safe delivery of children.

Why is there a roof over the sumo DOHYŌ?

Originally, the Shinto shrine-like roof had religious significance and also helped protect the ring from the elements. The roof was supported by four wooden pillars, each wrapped in differently colored cloth. In 1952, it was decided to remove the posts so that people in the increasingly distant seats would be able to see the *dohyō* action.

Why are there four colored tassels hanging from the roof of the DOHYŌ?

The four posts that formerly held up the roof were replaced with tassels of the same colors as those of

HINA DOLL

the posts. The tassel at the northeast corner is green, representing spring and the green dragon god of the East. The tassel at the southeast corner is red, representing summer and the deity of the South. The southwest tassel is white, representing autumn and the white tiger of the West. The northwest tassel is black, representing winter and the snake-encircled turtle god of the North.

Why do Japanese adorn their homes with DOLLS on stepped platforms?

The people of Heian Japan made paper dolls, stroked their bodies to transfer their sins and misfortunes to the dolls, and floated the dolls down a river in early March. At almost the same time, it became popular for court ladies to play with dolls, a custom that soon spread to the lower classes, as well. Eventually, these two customs came together, and during the Edo period the *hina-matsuri*, or Doll Festival, came to be celebrated on March 3. As doll displays grew more elaborate over the years, tiered stands gradually evolved for the dolls.

In the hina DOLL arrangement, why is the Empress on the right?

In Japanese tradition, the right side (as you face it) is superior to the left side. Kyoto-style dolls follow this tradition, with the Empress on the left, in deference to the Emperor. The opposite arrangement is called the Edo style. This alternate arrangement came about when the people of Edo decided to celebrate the fact that a "local" daughter, a great-granddaughter of Tokugawa Ieyasu, became empress. They were excited that one of their "own" had been accepted into the imperial family and arranged the dolls with the Empress in the superior position.

Why don't Japanese pour their own DRINKS?

After a few drinks among close friends, Japanese may well start filling their own glasses, but generally one only fills the glasses of other people. This is a form of social interaction, and by keeping an eye on the level of companions' glasses, one shows attentiveness and consideration for them. Almost invariably, a person for whom you pour will reciprocate by taking the bottle and pouring for you. This "tit-for-tat" pouring should not be taken as trying to put you under the table. If you are at the limit of your capacity, you need only sip from the refilled glass and set it down again. You will have participated in the ritual without endangering your health.

In Japan's thousands of "hostess clubs," the nicely dressed hostesses will, in addition to keeping the conversational ball rolling when necessary, assume responsibility for filling the glasses of the entire party. In the absence of hostesses, young women in the party will often assume this role.

Why *do* Japanese get **DRUNK** *so fast?*

Japanese (and American Indians) tend to have an increased level of an unusual enzyme which metabolizes alcohol unusually fast.

In short, the alcohol goes to work much faster in most Japanese than it does in most Caucasians. That, and the Japanese love of saké (20% alcohol) and whiskey (43% alcohol), creates an obvious and rapid cause-effect relationship. This is also thought to produce the characteristic "alcohol flush" experienced by about 80% of genetically Mongoloid individuals. Even despite the missing enzyme, however, there are Japanese who seem to possess an infinite capacity for alcohol and show no effects at all, no matter how much they drink.

Is *the* **EARPICK** *a Japanese invention?*

For those of us who were told as children never to stick anything other than our elbows into our ears, the sight of someone cleaning the ear canal with a narrow bamboo pick is unnerving, to say the least. It appears to be a tradition that came to Japan from China. The scene of a husband placing his head on the lap of his wife and having his ear cleaned is symbolic of domestic harmony in Japan; it can often be seen in kabuki plays and televised period dramas.

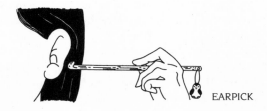

EARPICK

How does the Great Hanshin EARTHQUAKE of 1995 compare with the Great Kanto Earthquake of 1923 in terms of damage?

The destructive quake that struck the Awaji Island-Kobe-Osaka region in early 1995 resulted in the loss of over six thousand lives and tens of thousands of homes. As bad as this was, however, the Kanto quake ranks as one of the most destructive temblors in history, with 575,000 homes destroyed and nearly 143,000 people estimated killed.

Why is it customary to eat EEL in the heat of summer?

Japanese culture includes many customs related to the maintenance of good health, and one tradition that has continued to the present day is the consumption of eel in the heat of summer.

Not only is eel delicious, but it is rich in protein and therefore a healthy meal when served with rice. The traditional day for eating eel is called *doyō*, a day in late July or early August which is traditionally considered the hottest day of the year. It comes eighteen days prior to the traditional beginning of autumn. Few Japanese can tell you exactly when *doyō* will fall in a given year, but most calendars printed in Japan will remind them of this date that offers as good an excuse as any to enjoy eel. It is said that Hiraga Gennai, a naturalist and writer of the mid-Edo period, advertised the benefits of eating eel on this day in order to save eel restaurants from losing business in Japan's staggering summer heat.

Where is the fastest passenger ELEVATOR in Japan?

Not only the fastest in Japan, but currently the fastest in the world, the express elevators of the Yokohama

Landmark Tower in Yokohama zip up and down at a speed of 45 kph. Ascending from the second floor to the sixty-ninth floor takes a mere forty seconds.

Why do Japanese wear shirts with incoherent ENGLISH on them?

Japanese place nonsensical combinations of English words on shopping bags, T-shirts, jackets, notebooks, and many other products. English-speakers make the mistake of "reading" the words and trying to understand them. The designers who create the garbled texts do not intend for them to be "read" at all. The English words are only intended to be a component of a graphic design that is to be "looked at." Where an English-speaker might wear a bracelet with a hieroglyphic design that he or she cannot read, Japanese wear clothing and carry bags with "designs" that just happen to have (or, just as often, lack) meaning to other people.

Why do office and factory workers EXERCISE together before work?

For almost seventy years, NHK radio has broadcast an exercise program complete with instructions, rhythm, and counting. Tapes and CDs of this regular routine are also used in schools to make sure that students learn the routine of calisthenics. Some schools even require that pupils join in the 6:30 A.M. session at local parks during the summer vacation to prevent their lazing away because of the heat. Since virtually every Japanese is familiar with the routine, and employers want their workers to get off to a good start in the morning, companies often incorporate a shorter routine into the brief meetings that start the day. It must also be noted that being limber at the start of the day helps factory and construction workers avoid accidents.

What is the meaning of two successive sets of three loud FIRECRACKERS set off during the day and evening?

This is the standard way of announcing an upcoming festival or school field day. These booming fireworks make only brief flashes high in the sky before the sound travels to the neighboring area, reminding the local residents that something entertaining is going to take place.

Why do FIRETRUCKS drive through neighborhoods making announcements on winter nights?

Due to the particular dryness of Japanese winter months, the local fire brigades make their rounds reminding everyone to check that all sources of flame are extinguished before turning in, and to refrain from smoking in bed.

What makes Japanese FIREWORKS world-famous?

Let's be clear from the start: we are not talking about the kind of fireworks that children play with on hot summer evenings. We are dealing with the fireworks used in public displays. The kind that measure 8.5 to 100 centimeters in diameter and give off bursts of light that measure 60 to 600 meters in diameter.

What makes Japanese fireworks special is the fact that their explosions appear round from any angle. The fireworks of many other countries appear round from one side, but flat and tube-shaped from others. This unique attribute of Japanese fireworks is why

SHACHIHOKO

Japanese pyrotechnicians travel the world over to put on displays.

Like other works of art, these short-lived visual treats do not come cheap. According to fireworks producer Hosoya Enterprise, a 30-centimeter, hand-made, ball-shaped explosive will cost an average of ¥50,000 to ¥60,000. At prices like these, the Sumida River fireworks display in August runs well above ¥60 million for the explosives alone.

What are the FISH-like decorations on the tops of castles?

The gilt *shachihoko* resemble dolphins with large scales and their tails raised high above their heads. Originally, they were thought to have the power of preventing fire.

What's the only household FIXTURE honored with a holiday?

Although few Japanese perform any special functions for it, November 10 is the day that commemorates the humble toilet.

Why this date in particular? Because the numbers eleven and ten (11/10) can be broken down so that their component parts are read *to i i rei*, a collection of sounds nearly homophonic with *toire*, the Japanese word for "toilet").

What is the most often FORGOTTEN item in Japan?

According to police records, four hundred thousand umbrellas were turned in to police boxes across the nation in 1994. That adds up to three thousand umbrellas per rainfall. After umbrellas, the most turned-in items are, in descending order, credit and bank cards, wallets, clothing, and bags and briefcases. In addition, an astounding ¥2.8 billion was also turned in during that year, with about 73% being returned to the appropriate claimants. Another 20% went unclaimed and was eventually given to the persons who turned the money in.

What do you do with the FORTUNE lots you draw at certain temples?

At most shrines and temples, you can draw a *mikuji*, or "sacred lot," which tells you what to expect in the coming year. In some cases, one shakes a canister filled with numbered sticks until one of the sticks pops out of the small hole in the canister. Each stick's number corresponds to a number written on a paper fortune, and once a stick comes out of the canister, one takes the slip whose number corresponds to that of the stick. In other cases, one simply takes one of the lots in a large box. Everyone would like to draw a lot that says *daikichi*, *kichi*, or even *shōkichi*, meaning respectively "great fortune," "good fortune," and "small good fortune." If they can't manage any of these, though, and they draw one that says *kyō*, or "unlucky," then they should be careful and perhaps make an

even more enthusiastic request to the gods and buddhas for help in the coming months. Generally, these
lots are tied to the branches of trees on the grounds
of the shrine.

Why are there FOXES in front of shrines?

Like the *tanuki*, the fox has long been considered an
animal possessing supernatural powers, but the fox
is less amusing than fearsome. Stone foxes are often
found at the entrance to shrines venerating Inari, the
guardian god of cereal crops. In medieval times, the
white fox was believed to be sacred, and it came to be
regarded as the god's messenger.

Why is a piece of fried soybean curd (also called
inari) offered at the Inari shrine? Because it is believed to be the favorite food of the fox sentinel.

What do Japanese do in their FREE TIME?

A survey conducted by the Leisure Development Center in 1992 found that Japanese leisure activities differ considerably from those of Western nations. Only
about 49% of Japanese read as a hobby, while 19%
have an interest in photography, 8% entertain at home,
and 42% dine out regularly. By comparison, 66% of
Americans read, 29% are interested in photography,
30% entertain at home, and 60% enjoy dining out.

What activities are Japanese more likely to participate in? Golf is enjoyed by 16% of Japanese, while
40% devote time to domestic travel.

What do Japanese do when they enter their homes after attending a FUNERAL?

Mourners will usually sprinkle salt over themselves
and wash their hands, and some may even gargle to

purify themselves after being in contact with the impurity of death. After the funeral, mourners may be provided with a white handkerchief and a small packet of salt specifically for this purpose.

Why aren't FUNERALS held on auspicious days?

Of the six-day cycle of auspicious and inauspicious days found on many calendars, the auspicious day called *tomo-biki* is considered inappropriate for a funeral because of the idea that one might "pull a friend" (the phrase *tomodachi o hiku* contracts into *tomo-biki*) along into death. Whether or not the bereaved are personally concerned about observing such customs, chances are that they will avoid holding the funeral on this day to avoid offending those who attend.

Taking advantage of the general desire to avoid holding ceremonies on this day, crematoria and funeral services tend to shut down on these days, anyway, so it is virtually impossible to hold services even if one is inclined to do so. A new variation on "death taking a holiday," perhaps.

Why are most weddings Shintoist and FUNERALS Buddhist?

Japanese have traditionally believed that new relationships and undertakings should be begun under the guardianship of Shinto gods who can purify them. Along these lines, the beginning of construction of a new house, the celebration of a new birth in the family, and a wedding ceremony are all often accompanied by Shinto ritual.

Since Buddhism teaches the impermanence of all things, it is not designed for celebrating such ephemeral events. On the other hand, it is well-equipped to recognize the end of life as a transitory existence, whereas death is perceived as an impurity that does not jibe well with Shinto ceremonies because it can not be reversed, or, by extension, purified. As a result of this religious thinking, social custom has led Japanese to consider celebratory events as "belonging" to Shinto ceremonies and funeral ceremonies as "belonging" to Buddhist ceremonies.

Why do so many older people play "GATE BALL"?

During the hard-pressed days that followed the end of the war, a resident of Asahikawa, Hokkaido looked for a game that children could enjoy and that did not require expensive equipment or special facilities. He found that croquet fit these requirements, and all the necessary equipment could be made from lumber, one material that was not hard to come by in those days. With a new set of equipment and modified rules, he created "gate ball" in 1947.

Originally, the game was for children, but in the 1970s the game came to be promoted for seniors. In addition to getting older people outside, the game requires teamwork and headwork, giving it advantages on several different levels for older people. Today the game is enjoyed by an estimated 4 million players and has spread to some ten other nations.

Why are there huge GATES in front of shrines?

The gate-like structures called *torii* mark the sacred spaces of a shrine. There are usually two columns with a top rail and a second horizontal rail, but there is a theory that there were originally two columns with a horizontal rope joining them. The origin of the

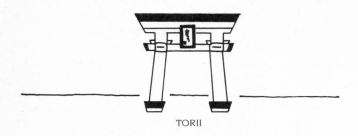

TORII

word *torii*, which is written with the characters "bird" and "perch," is rooted in the mythical episode in which Amaterasu hid herself in the cave. To augment the cheery noises which they made to try to lure the goddess out of her hiding place, the other deities collected birds and got them to sing. With this story in mind, people created a roosting place before the shrines to show that they are sacred.

Are GEISHA prostitutes? Are they still around? How can I meet one?

The true geisha is a highly trained professional artist who is hardly to be compared with a woman of loose virtue. She is usually trained in the playing of the koto and samisen, Japanese dance, and the wearing of kimono, in addition to the arts of conversation and games. Professional, full-time geisha do exist in Tokyo, Kyoto, and a few other major cities, but you will rarely meet one unless a wealthy friend or business acquaintance arranges for one to appear at a party or business function. Getting true geisha to appear cannot be arranged without proper introductions, and the fees are astronomical. Ersatz geisha, who are non-professional, and/or part-time entertainers, accept engagements at events such as parties at numerous hot springs, and are less highly trained, but their availability may be no greater than that of their professional, urban counterparts.

Do Japanese GHOSTS have legs?

Japanese ghosts once had legs, but as early as the Heian period Buddhist priests, aided by screens depicting the horrors of hell, spread the view that by the time the dead passed the third of the ten judges of hell they lost their legs and were left with transparent, shadowy appendages. Still, ghosts in popular folklore maintained their legs until some two hundred fifty years ago, when stories and paintings began to depict ghosts with shadowy arms limp at the wrist, and no legs at all.

What gifts are popular for the semiannual seasonal GIFT seasons?

Department stores set up special displays in June for summer gifts and in November for year-end gifts. The perennial favorites are green or black tea, dried seaweed, coffee, jam, meats, fish, cheese and butter, juice, canned fruit, soy sauce, wine, whiskey, beer, cookies, candy, bath soap, towels, and gift certificates. Prices normally range from ¥3,000 to ¥5,000 per gift.

What happened to GINKAKUJI'S silver leaf?

Visitors to Kyoto almost invariably visit Kinkakuji, or the Temple of the Golden Pavilion, in the north part of the city and Ginkakuji, or the Temple of the Silver Pavilion, in the eastern part. The contrast between the brilliant, gold leaf-covered Golden Pavilion and the dull, natural wood exterior of the Silver Pavilion is memorable. It is also, of course, surprising, given the name of the latter temple.

Inspired by Kyoto's spectacular Temple of the Golden Pavilion, Shogun Ashikaga Yoshimasa decided to attempt a similar feat in the eastern hills of the city with Ginkakuji. Unfortunately, at the time of his death in 1479, construction had not yet advanced to the silver leaf stage. Yoshimasa's heirs apparently never saw fit to add the final exterior decoration, and so the temple has remained ungilt to this day, although the name "Silver Pavilion" has stuck.

Where did Tokyo's GINZA get its name?

The characters used to write the name of this shopping and entertainment center of downtown Tokyo are *gin*, or "silver," and *za*, or "mint." It is named for the mint that the Tokugawa government set up there in 1612 for producing silver coins. It remained there for nearly two centuries, until the government decided in 1800 to move it to the other side of Nihonbashi.

Who was the first person in Japan to wear GLASSES?

Catholic missionary Saint Francis Xavier is reported to have introduced the first eyeglasses to Japan in 1551. The oldest extant pair are a tortoise-shell-rimmed pince-nez used by Tokugawa Ieyasu, progenitor of the Tokugawa shogunate (1600-1868).

Why do politicians wear white GLOVES when they campaign?

Every politician would like to impress the voters with how "clean" his hands are amidst universal rumors of corruption, hence the white cotton gloves.

Why are inexpensive cotton GLOVES called "army hands"?

The term *gunte*, or "army hands," is a short form of the term *gunyō te-bukuro*, or "gloves for military use." During the Russo-Japanese War of 1904–5, gloves were in great demand, in both the military and manufacturing sectors. To simplify the issuing of gloves, someone came up with the idea of making them so that one size fit all. In addition, the gloves were made so that they could be worn on either hand, eliminating the need to replace an entire pair when only one glove was worn out or lost.

Japan produces 60 million dozen white *gunte* and another 3.5 million dozen of the dyed, elastic variety every year. She imports another eight hundred thousand dozen or more from other nations of Asia. Annual domestic sales of these multipurpose gloves amount to approximately six pairs per person.

Why do Japanese say GOCHISŌSAMA after a meal?

If we remove the honorifics *go-* and *-sama* from the word, we are left with *chisō*, or "run quickly." By extension, the word has come to express gratitude to the host or cook for "running around here and there," collecting the ingredients and preparing them for the meal.

Did the GODDESS of Mercy originally start out as a goddess?

One of the most popular bodhisattvas in Japanese Buddhism, Kannon is the personification of compassion and is believed to deliver all beings from their sufferings. Known as Avalokitesvara in India, Kannon was originally male, but underwent a transformation to female form as Buddhism spread out from India, across Asia. Visit the Sanjusangendo in Kyoto to see the 1,001 statues of the Thousand-Armed Kannon, and you will be able to decide for yourself which form Kannon takes in this country.

How did GOLF get started in Japan?

An English tea merchant, Arthur H. Groom, is credited with introducing golf to Japan in 1901. With several friends, he built the first golf course in Kobe, and two years later he established Japan's first golf club there. In 1906, foreigners established another beachhead for the game, this time in Yokohama, and the following year, the First Japan Amateur Golfers' Championship Tournament was played between the Kobe and Yokohama clubs. The first golf club to be established by Japanese was established in Komazawa, Tokyo in 1914, and it hosted the Twelfth Amateur Golfers' Championship Tournament—its first time hosting the event—in 1918. Spurred by a Japanese golfer's victory in the tournament, golf's popularity among Japanese rose sharply thereafter, retaining its wide following to the present day.

What is a "G PAN"?

A "G pan" really isn't a pan at all, but an article of clothing. Japanese call blue jeans G *pan* from combining and truncating the English words "jeans" and "pants."

Why do visitors to graves sprinkle water over the GRAVESTONES?

In addition to making the stone look nicer, this practice is considered a form of purification.

Is Japan's population "GRAYING" faster than those of other nations?

When 7% of the population of a nation is over sixty-five years old, it is called an "aging" society by sociologists. When 14% of the population is over sixty-five years old, it is said to constitute an "aged" society. Whereas it took France, for instance, 115 years for the number of people over sixty-five to rise from 7% to 14% of the total population, it is likely to take Japan only twenty-four years to cover the same ground. In 1993, 13.5% of the population of Japan was over sixty-five years old, and it is estimated that that percentage will climb to 25% in the next thirty years. This rapid growth of the elderly segment of the population will make Japan the fastest-aging nation in the world. Two reasons for this phenomenon are Japan's low birthrate (an average of 1.5 children per family in 1992) and the fact that its people enjoy the longest life expectancy in the world.

Why are the deluxe cars on the bullet trains called "GREEN cars"?

JR East Japan explains that the colors green and orange are simply good "image" colors. As a result, we have the "green car," where seating is more luxurious, the "green window," where seat reservations are handled and long-distance train tickets are sold, orange prepaid fare cards, and JR's green Yamanote Line and orange Chuo Line.

Why do your HANDS turn yellow when you eat too many mikan?

You need not be alarmed or embarrassed by this symptom. It does not mean that your eyes are going, or that you need to wash your hands with stronger soap. The yellowness is not on the surface of your hands, but beneath their skin.

When you eat a few too many *mikan*, your body absorbs that much more carotene, an orange pigment which is then passed through your blood. Because the palms of your hands have less of the pigment called melanin than do other parts of your body, the skin is more transparent, and the orange-yellow substance in the bloodstream is more apparent. The same effect is brought on by eating pumpkins or carrots, but in Japan one more often tends to eat *mikan*, resulting in this seasonal "change of color."

Why do Japanese play HANETSUKI at New Year's?

This traditional game, which resembles badminton, is played with a wooden paddle and a brightly feathered shuttlecock. When one person plays, the person simply tries to keep the shuttlecock in the air. When two people play, the game resembles badminton, except with no net. The original meaning of the game concerned enabling its player(s) to avoid the bite of the mosquito in the year to come. The shuttlecock resembles a dragonfly, and everyone knows that drag-

HANETSUKI

onflies are helpful in decreasing the mosquito population. Therefore, one's protection from the troublesome insect grows in proportion to the length of time
that the shuttlecock stays in the air.

Why do drivers turn their HEADLIGHTS off when they stop at intersections?

We once heard a non-Japanese venture that Japanese
drivers did this to prevent unnecessary wear on the
car battery, but that is not the reason. It is simply a
matter of etiquette. When stopped at a light, you do
not need your headlights on, and turning them off
prevents glare in other drivers' eyes. Come to think of
it, why do people in other countries leave them on at
intersections?

Why are there "HEALTH DRINKS" targeted at children?

Just like their stressed-out businessmen fathers, Japanese children put in long, hard days. A normal routine might include a full day at school, after-school
activities, and evening "cram" school, before return-
ing home to do homework. As a result of their preparations for entrance examinations at various stages
in their young lives, kids complain of eyestrain, dull-
ness, irritability, and general exhaustion. To meet the
needs of these beleaguered boys and girls, the major
"health drink" manufacturers in the early 1990s began
to produce special, decaffeinated "drinks" concocted
specifically for children.

Where did the reign name "HEISEI" come from?

The Japanese calendar's system of using period names
began in the year 645, and names were changed when-

ever the capital moved or some other major event took place. Today, however, the name changes with the accession of a new emperor. The current era name comes from the Chinese *Book of Documents* and *Records Compiled by the Historian*. The first character, *hei*, means "peace" and is used for the twenty-fourth time out of a total of 247 era names. The second character, *sei*, is used for the first time in history and means "achieving" in this context.

Is *the* HI-NO-MARU *Japan's national flag?*

The rising sun flag has been in service since at least the thirteenth century, and by the Edo period it flew from all Japanese ships. It has come into use on land, as well, although it is still heatedly protested in places such as Okinawa when it is flown at official gatherings and school events. The so-called Rising Sun flag with sixteen rays is a military service flag (still used today by Japan's Self-Defense Forces), and has never been an official national flag. The crimson disc on a white field that is used as Japan's de facto national flag has also never been officially designated as the national flag, although custom, if not law, has established that place for it both inside and outside of the country.

Why is there a HOLIDAY on April 29?

From its name of *midori no hi*, or "Green Day," one might assume that the Japanese national holiday had something to do with spring leaves. Actually, it was a holiday to commemorate the birthday of the Showa Emperor, also known as Emperor Hirohito. With his passing, the day was kept as a holiday but under a different name. The holiday got its new name (before the monarch died, it had simply been referred to as "the Emperor's birthday") from the sovereign's high regard for and interest in nature.

What time of the day is called the "correct hour of the HORSE"?

The kanji used to mean "correct" also carries a connotation of "main." For instance, it is used in the Sino-Japanese term for "main entrance." Because noon is right in the middle of the day, and an important point of time reference, it also came to be associated with this character. Before the introduction of the clock and the modern concept of the twenty-four-hour day, the Japanese used a system of telling time that divided the day into twelve periods, one for each animal in the Chinese zodiac. The period from sunrise to sunset was divided into six periods, with the period including noon being designated the "hour of the horse." For this reason, noon is still called *shōgo*, or the "correct hour of the horse."

Why should you not take potted flowers to someone in the HOSPITAL?

Potted plants inauspiciously suggest that a long stay in the hospital is imminent. One should also avoid offering flowers in fours and nines, because homonyms for these numbers in Japanese include words for "death" and "suffering," respectively.

Why are the baths for men at HOT SPRINGS larger than those for women?

Until the recent boom in hot spring-hopping among coeds and female office workers, it was more often men who went off to these resorts on company trips and for "entertainment." The size of the men's common bath was therefore larger, offering more spigots and larger tubs. Increasing numbers of female guests, however, are inducing inns and other lodgings at hot springs to build their baths to at least equal size when they renovate.

Why are there often big year-end HOUSECLEAN-INGS?

December 13 is considered to be the beginning of the New Year season, and traditionally the house was to be cleaned on this day in preparation for the arrival of the god of the New Year. The religious significance attending this grand event has grown very feeble, but the feeling that a thorough dusting and cleaning is important for starting the year fresh remains very strong. For convenience, this cleaning is often postponed until after the company vacations have started at year's end. The annual cleaning extends even to the giant statue of the Buddha at Nara and the other shrines and temples where visitors will come to worship at the New Year.

What two intruders have the Imperial Household Agency been unable to keep out of the IMPERIAL PALACE grounds?

Like most urban residents, the keepers of the grounds have been unable to prevent intrusions by crows or cats.

What are the three IMPERIAL REGALIA?

The authority of the imperial household is symbolized by the three sacred treasures, or imperial regalia. A curved jewel, mirror, and sword are held to have been passed down from the Sun Goddess Amaterasu through successive generations of the imperial household all the way to the present emperor. Atsuta Shrine in Nagoya is believed to hold the sacred sword, which the brother of Amaterasu is recorded as having taken from an enormous serpent. The sacred mirror is thought to be in the Ise Shrine in Mie Prefecture. The sacred jewel, and replicas of the other two treasures, are believed to be in the possession of the Imperial Palace in Tokyo.

Were the compact disc player and the video tape recorder INVENTED in Japan?

Neither of these items for whose manufacture Japan is famous was invented by Japanese. The floppy disk, however, is the brainchild of the eccentric Japanese inventor Yoshiro Nakamatsu—better known to the world as "Doctor NakaMats"—who holds a large number of patents.

Why do the buildings at the "ancient" ISE Grand Shrine look so new?

Ise Grand Shrine is actually a complex of many structures where the Sun Goddess Amaterasu has been worshipped for almost seventeen centuries. The central structure of the Inner Shrine is situated on one of two identical, contiguous lots, one of which is always kept empty. Every twenty years a new structure is built on the unoccupied lot. Once the new building is complete, the deity is transferred to the new building, the older building is demolished, and the old lot is left empty for the next twenty years. As a result, this most sacred of shrines is never more than twenty years old. This tradition of rebuilding once a generation guarantees that when the time to rebuild comes, the specially designated carpenters, smiths, and other craftsmen can count on the knowledge and experience of those who worked on the previous reconstruction.

Are all J-LEAGUE players professionals?

No, the league allows amateur players to compete as full members of the pro teams. In all likelihood, such a player would be an employee of the parent company that owns the team.

What color belt does an expert JUDOIST wear?

If you guessed black, then try again. People at the apex of the judo pyramid, holders of ninth- and tenth-degree master rankings, are entitled to wear scarlet belts. Holders of sixth- through eighth-degree master rankings may wear scarlet-and-white striped belts. First- through fifth-degree holders wear black. Below the master rankings are the "regular" ranks, whose insignia belts are, in descending order, brown (purple for children) and white.

Never seen a judo master in anything but a black belt? Many masters, although entitled to wear the higher colors, opt for the traditional black instead.

Why are all KABUKI actors male?

Ironically, the inventor of kabuki is believed to have been a female attendant at the Grand Izumo Shrine in Shimane Prefecture. With a troupe of mostly women, she put on performances of dance and comedy in the dry riverbed of the Kamogawa River in Kyoto in 1603. As years passed, these performances became more sensual, and the entertainers also began to offer their

KABUKI

"services" after the shows, so the Tokugawa shogunate banned women from appearing in the popular entertainments. Similar problems developed when the attractive young male actors who took over the roles of women also sold their favors, but somehow that didn't provoke such a scandal: kabuki since the mid-seventeenth century has used only male actors.

When did KANA come into use?

Ideographic characters, or kanji, were introduced to Japan from China. During the Heian period, women developed their own cursive way of writing these characters; this developed over time into what we know now as hiragana. Shortly thereafter, the more angular katakana appeared as a convenient form of shorthand for students studying Buddhist thought. Both scripts have their roots in truncations or simplifications of Chinese characters.

Where did the sponge cake called KASUTERA come from?

Among the items and customs that the Portuguese introduced to Nagasaki during the years prior to the Edo period was a type of sweet sponge cake. This cake became widely popular at the beginning of Edo and remains so today. The Spanish name Castilla, via Portuguese, became *kasutera* in Japanese, and that is the name by which it is still known.

Does KENDO *have black belts?*

Unlike most of the martial arts, kendo does not have an obvious sign for ranked participants. The standard clothing may have the person's name and affiliation, but there is no way to discern a participant's rank from attire alone. When practicing in the dojo, the instructors usually line up on one side, the learners on the other: the side with fewer practitioners is invariably the instructors' side.

Where did the KEWPIE *doll come from?*

The earliest Kewpies appeared in a 1909 edition of the *Ladies Home Journal* in the United States. Once popular in the U.S. in the form of bisque dolls, they became popular in Japan first in celluloid form, and then in the form of soft plastic. The licensing rights were bought, and are still held, by a Japanese mayonnaise maker which took its name from the baby-faced doll. Kewpies also appear in advertisements and are the mascot for a major bank. Toy manufacturers still produce the dolls in both unclothed form and with full wardrobes, Asian and Western.

What is "KEY MONEY" *for?*

At the commencement of a lease agreement for land or housing, the landlord may require both a rental deposit equivalent to several months' rent, and a specified amount of "key money." The former must be returned to the lessor at the expiration of the lease, although the landlord may deduct a sum for damage or unpaid rent. The latter is a "gift" that is not returned at the end of the lease. The practice of requiring these fees has no basis in law. Nevertheless, if the landlord requires either or both of these, the lessee has no choice but to pay them if he or she really wants to rent the property. The landlord unilaterally sets the amounts required for each.

Do women traditionally wear underwear beneath KIMONO?

Proper Japanese girls wear underwear beneath their kimono. Improper Japanese girls, who are much more fun, however, do not. The official line is that one shouldn't: the show-through outline spoils the smoothness of the fabric.

How old is KINKAKUJI?

Perhaps the most famous structure in Japan, the gilded pavilion of Kinkankuji, the Temple of the Golden Pavilion, was built by the Shogun Ashikaga Yoshimitsu (1358–1408). Amazingly, it survived the vast destruction of the Onin War (1467–1477), numerous fires and earthquakes, and the more recent Pacific War. Unfortunately, it became the object of obsession of a deranged monk, who burned the place to the ground in 1950. The "ancient" pavilion is an exact replica and dates from 1955.

Do KOKESHI dolls represent unwanted children?

There are several theories concerning the origin of the simple, cylindrical wooden dolls produced in great abundance in the Tohoku region. One of them is that long ago when mere survival was quite difficult, in-

KOKESHI

fanticide was not unknown, and these simple dolls were made to appease the spirits of the unfortunate newborns. There is no conclusive evidence supporting this or other theories.

Why is KYOTO *carefully laid out in square blocks?*

Unlike Tokyo and almost every other Japanese city, Kyoto is an easy city to negotiate because of its straight roads and rectangular shape. When it was established in the year 794 under the name Heiankyo, Kyoto was built along a plan based on the Chinese city of Chang An, capital of China's Tang Dynasty (618–907). Its location was selected in accordance with the laws of Chinese geomancy; its design was based on the Chinese capital, because Japan's leaders, who wished to emulate the grandest city that they knew, looked to a China that held overpowering cultural sway over the Japan of that time.

Do all KYOTO *fishermen use bait and tackle?*

Primarily to delight tourists, fishermen in Kyoto, Gifu, and several other areas catch fish in local rivers with the assistance of a dozen or so trained cormorants. Fishing at night, the fishermen attract fish with light from torches hung out over the surface of the water. The fishermen then place constrictive collars around the necks of the cormorants, the actual fishers in this enterprise, to prevent them from actually swallowing the fish they catch. A line is attached to each of the birds, and they are set to work. When a bird is successful, its handler pulls it in, takes away what should be its rightful reward, and puts it back to work.

Why is soup served in LACQUER bowls?

In a Japanese-style meal, soup is served in a bowl which a person picks up and drinks directly from. The ideal bowl should be light, strong, able to maintain the heat of the soup without becoming hot in the hand, and have a smooth edge from which to drink. Lacquer bowls satisfy all these conditions. Soup is often served in a bowl with a lid, and on occasion the pressure under the lid creates a vacuum-like lock. To release the pressure, firmly but gently press the sides of the bowl together.

CORMORANT FISHING

Why are LANTERNS set afloat on rivers and the ocean?

On the first night of the Bon festival in August, particularly in rural areas, families place paper lanterns painted with their surnames in front of their homes to welcome the spirits of their ancestors. After their annual visit to the family home, the ancestral spirits return to the other world, and family members help guide them by setting small floats with paper lanterns on top and lighted candles inside afloat on nearby rivers, lakes, or bays. Not to greet and send off the ancestors' spirits properly would invite trouble.

One of the largest of these observances is in Matsushima Bay in Miyagi Prefecture, where the event has become a major tourist attraction. Kyoto has its own variation of this send-off, as well. Huge kanji and other figures are plotted out on the slopes of five mountains ringing the city. Stacks of wood are then laid out at intervals along the lines of these figures, and when they are lit on the evening of August 16, the figures can be seen all over the city.

What does a red diagonal line across a LICENSE PLATE mean?

Since automobiles are licensed by the national government, there are few variations in automobile license plates. Ordinary private vehicles have green characters on white backgrounds, and commercial vehicles have the reverse combination. Yellow-and-black combinations are for small-displacement vehicles. The diagonal red line? It is a temporary license plate which may be attached by an auto dealer for a test drive. Otherwise, it may indicate that the owner of the vehicle carelessly forgot to get his car inspected in time; he has applied to the local government office for permission to drive to the inspection station and received that temporary plate.

What is the meaning of a backlighted LICENSE PLATE?

There is no special meaning. Some car owners think they look snazzy, and the licensing bureau has no particular objections to them. All such plates start with katakana *ro* or *ru*.

Why are public LOTTERY tickets sold by a private bank? And why only one?

Dai-Ichi Kangyo Bank, Ltd is entrusted with sales of lottery tickets and the distribution of prize monies because it seems to have mastered the art of profiting from the business. Legally, any bank can apply to the government for the right to manage a lottery, but only Dai-Ichi Kangyo seems to have the skill to make it worth their while to operate the business. What is it worth to the bank? It receives operating expenses ranging from 9% per ¥100 ticket to 6% per ¥300 ticket.

How large is the clientele of the "LOVE HOTELS"?

According to figures for 1993, there were thirty thousand of these institutions in Japan, with an average of twenty rooms per establishment. Reports show that each room is occupied by two or three couples per day. By putting these figures together, we come to a total of 2 million guests per day.

Why are MAILBOXES red?

The Ministry of Posts and Telecommunications says that the first mailbox was a white, wooden box set up in 1871. This was followed by a black box and then the first red mailbox at Nihonbashi in 1901. They finally settled on the red box because it stood out.

What is the proper way to eat a MANDARIN orange?

Yes, the Japanese even have a proper way to eat the humble *mikan*. If you want to impress others with your good manners, be sure to peel the fruit downward from the place where the stem was attached, parting the skin into four sections. Leave the bottom intact. That way you will have a receptacle for the parts that you leave uneaten. Remove one section and, holding the innermost edge, pull the meat out with your teeth. Place the remaining skin of the section back into the peel. After you have eaten the contents, you can pull the peel over the top so that the remains will not be visible.

One apocryphal story of an *o-miai*, a formal meeting in which prospective marriage partners are introduced, describes the discussion between a young man and his mother that follows a meeting with a prospective bride. He is obviously attracted to the young woman, but his mother is dead set against the match. The disappointed son asks why she is so sure that the match would not be good, and the mother replies, "Because of the way she peeled her *mikan*." This is serious business.

What percentage of MARRIAGES are by arrangement?

According to a 1992 white paper on the subject by the Economic Planning Agency, love is in the air. Arranged marriages accounted for almost 37% of all marriages in 1973, but that figure fell to 13% in 1991.

So-called love marriages, in which the couple met on their own, resulted primarily from meeting on the job (35%) or through friends (26%). Despite the transition to do-it-yourself proposals, however, it remains customary to ask someone to serve as go-between, or *nakōdo*, during the wedding ceremony and subsequent reception.

How much money should one give to a couple getting MARRIED?

As in the West, the amount depends on the circumstances. In Japan, the deciding factors are one's relationship to the couple and whether or not one attends the wedding reception. If not attending the reception, a friend of middle age would give the couple ¥10,000. If attending the reception, the same friend would offer an envelope containing ¥30,000 to help offset the function's cost. With the exception of immediate family members and relatives, people not attending the reception will usually give between ¥5,000 and ¥30,000. The range for those attending the reception would be between ¥10,000 (a very low figure) and ¥30,000.

Why do Japanese sometimes wear surgical MASKS on the street?

Because of severe traffic congestion on Japanese streets and roads, the vast majority of people commute to work and school by public transportation. Some considerate people, when sick, wear these masks to try to prevent communicating their illnesses to other people through sneezing or coughing. A mask also protects its wearer from breathing in cold air during the winter. Still another benefit provided by masks, as well as glasses with frames that fit tightly around the face, is filtration of the pollen that causes hay fever.

Why are MATSUTAKE mushrooms so expensive?

Matsutake mushrooms elegantly arranged in a hand-woven bamboo basket fetch upward of ¥10,000 in an average year, while a larger package of *shiitake* mushrooms goes for ¥250. The reason for this is that the *matsutake* is the only commonly sold mushroom that cannot be cultivated. So far, no one has been able to determine everything that's necessary for getting it to grow properly under artificial conditions.

Why do some MELONS sell for ¥10,000?

Probably, very few of the astoundingly expensive fruits such as these melons find their way into the homes of the people actually purchasing them. These are almost invariably wrapped in cushioned boxes and used as gifts to express gratitude for considerations or assistance received. The recipient will know immediately that he or she has received a gift of value.

Do Japanese consider MICE pests?

Though you might not want him in your house, the friendly mouse is a symbol of abundance. After all, would he be staying at your house if there weren't enough to eat?

Why does such a large portion of the populace think they are MIDDLE-CLASS?

In a 1993 survey carried out by the Prime Minister's Office, 90% of the people of Japan responded that they thought of themselves as middle-class.

On the surface, it appears that there is little class consciousness in Japanese society. But the questions to which people responded actually dealt with where they felt were "in relation to others in society." If one associated primarily with people of similar income and property, then of course one would reply that one was in the "middle," regardless of whether this is really "middle-class."

A more telling breakdown is how many people felt themselves to be in the "upper middle class," "intermediate middle class," and "lower middle class." Responses in these categories totaled up to 11.1%, 54.6%, and 24.3%, respectively.

Want a quick guide to judging the economic status of your Japanese friends? The most reliable indicator is floor space of residence. A Home Economics Research Institute survey showed that those who thought they were lower-middle-class had homes with floor space of less than 50 square meters. The middle-middle groups had homes of 75 square meters. These are figures for urban residences; people in rural areas, where homes are bigger, probably have different standards.

Why shouldn't you MIX your unagi (eel) with your umeboshi (pickled plum)?

In the days before refrigeration and scientific knowledge of the causes of food-related gastric complaints, popular wisdom concerning combinations of foods that should be avoided was passed on by word of mouth. Beginning in about the fourteenth century, these prohibitions against combining such foods as eel and pickled plum, or tempura and watermelon became widespread, and although such beliefs have no scientific basis, members of the older generation even today believe that they should be avoided.

Why is the MOCHI served at the Doll Festival three-colored?

Around five hundred years ago, March 3 became a day to display dolls in what is now called the Doll Festival, and people placed various types of offerings in front of the displayed dolls. This being a time (according to the old calendar) when peach blossoms bloom, snow is still on the mountaintops, and green grass is sprouting in the fields, the tricolored *hishimochi* came to be made in those colors.

Where do the plastic MODELS of food in front of restaurants come from?

Glass cases displaying perfect models of cups of coffee, hamburger steaks, and spaghetti being lifted by a fork hanging in mid-air can be bought in the stores of Kappabashi in Tokyo. These realistic plastic-and-wax models, which look like food and taste like plastic, come very close to epitomizing the motto "what you see is what you get."

Why do Japanese say MOSHI MOSHI when answering the telephone?

When telephones were first introduced, a person would answer the phone with the rather rough phrase Oi oi, something like "Hey, Hey!" The caller would reply by saying Hai, *yō gozaimasu*, a humble way of saying "Yes, I've a matter [to discuss]." Gradually, this was replaced by Mōshimasu mōshimasu, or "I am going to say something," which was then in turn shortened to the current *moshi moshi*.

What is a "MOUNTAIN WHALE"?

The euphemism *yama-kujira* was applied to the meat of wild boar during the days when Buddhism prohibited the eating of animal flesh but allowed the eating of whale meat as "fish."

When did the custom of exchanging NAME cards begin?

Name cards, or *meishi*, are among the essentials of Japanese social relationships. The original Japanese version was made of handmade Japanese paper and contained merely the name of the presenter, written with brush and ink. The first Japanese to use printed cards were state officials who dealt with people from the West toward the end of the Edo period. Today, of course, a card contains all the various addresses and means of contacting its presenter, along with the all-important notation of the person's status.

What is considered when Japanese choose NAMES for their children?

In addition to taking characters from parents' or ancestors' names, Japanese also check the number of strokes in potential names. The rules for selecting auspicious names and avoiding inauspicious names are complex enough to warrant the publication of many books for that purpose. As in other cultures, there are trends in naming, and every year there seems to be a boom in one or another name. For 1994, the most popular girls' name was Ayaka, a name that can be written in twenty-seven different ways using kanji and kana. The next names, in descending order of popularity, were Haruka, Mai, Natsumi, and Misaki. In addition, because of the marriage of the Crown Prince to the former Owada Masako, the use of the final "-ko" (written with the character for "child") in names has enjoyed a revival.

Why are there so many police at NARITA Airport?

First, a bit of history. The ground upon which the New Tokyo International Airport was constructed belonged previously to Japanese who had returned from Manchuria in the wake of Japan's defeat in World War II. This land had been given to them as part of the postwar Japanese government's effort to absorb the thousands of returnees who descended upon the defeated nation.

When the people who received the land first took it over, the quality of the soil was very poor. Over time, however, they slowly built up the fertility of the land and became able to support themselves. Just as the residents of Narita had finally become able to earn decent livings from their homesteads, however, the government selected Narita as the site of a new international airport. The residents felt the government's action arbitrary and high-handed, especially considering that it had itself granted the land in the first place. This feeling of having been wronged led them, supported by radical students, to vigorously protest the construction. The government responded with extremely tight security, basing thousands of riot police on the site. Despite the government's forceful stand, however, radicals managed to get into the main control tower and severely damage its equipment just prior to the grand opening of the airport.

In the end, the entire saga continued for nearly a decade, from the commencement of construction in 1969, to the beginning of the airport's operation in

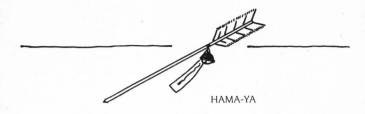

HAMA-YA

1978. Moreover, even now, although the airport has generally operated smoothly, protests and security have remained news items over the years.

Why do Japanese buy arrows at NEW YEAR'S?

When people make their first visit to a shrine at New Year's, they often buy an arrow talisman, called *hama-ya*, which is believed to destroy evil and prevent disasters. It is also thought to bring swift news of good fortune.

What are the most auspicious things to dream about on NEW YEAR'S?

The dream you have on the night of January 2 is called *hatsuyume*, the first dream of the new year. The people of Edo made much of this dream and sought to have lucky visions to bring them good fortune in the coming year. The three best things for *hatsuyume* were considered to be Mt. Fuji, a hawk, or an eggplant. These three objects were associated with the Suruga area (now Shizuoka Prefecture), the home of Tokugawa Ieyasu, who established the Tokugawa regime at the beginning of the seventeenth century. Obviously, the townspeople hoped that they might have the same good fortune as the mighty Ieyasu.

At first glance, it may seem odd that the "first" dream of the year was considered to be had on January 2. The reason for this line of thinking was that Edo people were not able to properly think about their dreams on the first night because of being tired from preparing for the New Year. So, they pushed the date for *hatsuyume* up by one day.

How many NEW YEAR'S greeting cards do Japanese send?

New Year's cards, or *nengajō*, date from 1874, only three years after the establishment of the Japanese postal service. At present, they account for almost one-fifth of all annual postal service revenues.

The postal service sold 37 billion greeting cards for the 1995 season, which amounts to an average of thirty cards per Japanese man, woman, and child. A family of four might be expected to send one hundred to one hundred fifty cards, while someone who is eager to maintain connections, business or otherwise, might fire off some three to four hundred.

NENGAJO

What is so special about NEW YEAR'S foods?

Collectively called *o-sechi-ryōri*, each of the foods eaten during the New Year holidays has some symbolic meaning. Herring roe, for instance, is eaten in the hope of having many descendants, represented by the large number of eggs that herring lay. Black beans are eaten because black is considered a charm for the exorcism of evil. Chestnuts symbolize hopes for wealth and prosperity because of their goldish-yellow coloring. Due to their shape, shrimp symbolize good health even into old age when the back is curled and bent.

Why are temple bells rung 108 times at NEW YEAR'S?

New Year's Eve is a very quiet time in Japan, and no matter where you are, as midnight approaches and the New Year arrives, you will hear Buddhist temple bells begin to ring. The bells are struck 108 times—once for each suffering that afflicts human beings in this world according to Buddhism. Striking a bell, according to tradition, extinguishes these sufferings one at a time. This, then, enables us to start out the new year with a fresh spirit. Better than a hangover!

Why do Japanese go to Shinto shrines at NEW YEAR'S?

Japanese pay a first visit to a shrine at the beginning of the new year to pray for the well-being of their families, success in school entrance exams in the coming twelve months, or even success in finding marriage partners. They may also visit Buddhist temples, especially major ones, in the hope that the Buddha will hear their prayers for a good year. These visits usually commence after 12 A.M. of January 1, and they are generally completed within the first few days of January.

How were NINJA *able to leap up onto the top of walls?*

Talented though many ninja were, they were not superhuman, though they may have appeared that way. Among the equipment a ninja would employ was a small springboard, which he would position along his planned escape route in case he should be in a rush to leave a scene quickly. Since ninja liked to work under cover of night, pursuers might not detect the springboard until it was too late, and an intruding ninja would already have bounded up to the top of the surrounding wall, ready to escape. In the movies, of course, the ninja just seems to rocket himself up on his own power.

Does the Emperor slurp his NOODLES in the traditional way?

The Emperor definitely does *not* slurp his noodles. No cultivated Japanese emits the slightest slurp eating noodles. The only people who do so are the boors one sits next to on planes and in déclassé restaurants.

What part of the house should not be on the NORTHEAST side?

It has long been held that one should not construct toilets or baths on the northeast side, as the northeast is considered an inauspicious direction. Further, the southeast side was considered best for wells and gates. However, during the postwar construction boom, and with the rapid rise in land prices, necessity has forced most people to overlook such considerations when planning their houses, deemphasizing tradition, in favor of economy.

Who works more OVERTIME, Japanese or Americans?

Although it is difficult to get figures for each nation that include the same types of workers doing the same types of jobs, the Japanese government White Paper on Labor says that, at least as of 1991, Japanese do put in more hours than Americans. Total actual working hours were 2,080 for Japan and 1,943 for the U.S. Total overtime working hours were 204 for Japan and 187 for the U.S. However, it is unclear how many hours of "informal," unpaid overtime are being worked in each country, and so these figures are useful only up to a point. Productivity, too, is another story.

How much can a professional PACHINKO player earn in a month?

According to Eric Sedensky (Winning Pachinko, Yen-books), a pro on a "digital pachinko," or deji-pachi, machine will spend from ¥20,000 to ¥100,000 on balls and take home between ¥40,000 and ¥150,000 a day. Given that even a pro will not spend seven days a week on the job, the average take-home income per month is probably about ¥500,000.

Why do PACHINKO winners trade pachinko balls for ordinary objects like packs of pens?

People play pachinko not only for the pleasure of watching the lights go on and off and hearing the steel balls rattle through the machines, but because there are prizes that can be won in exchange for the balls one has accumulated. At the exchange counter, a customer drops balls that have been won into an automatic counting machine and takes a card or slip of paper that shows the final tally of balls accumulated. These can then be exchanged for cigarettes, canned goods, soap, kitchen items, and sweets on the premises. Many winners, however, will exchange their balls for "exchange items," or *ryōgaehin*, such as lighter flints, packs of pens, and key chains. Since it is illegal to gamble for money, the pachinko parlor cannot exchange balls for money right then and there. The parlors get around this minor technicality by establishing "exchange booths," or *ryōgaejo*, where patrons can exchange their hard-won packs of pens or whatnot for cash. Regular patrons know where this small hole in the wall is, and although the exchange is not legal, the police and everyone else can tell what's going on.

Where did PACHINKO come from?

Ironically, the famous Japanese form of pinball came originally from the Corinthian Game developed in the United States. The object of this simple children's game was to shoot a small ball up to the top of a slightly inclined horizontal board and get it to land in one of the holes cut into the board. It was first used by Japanese candy store owners in the 1920s to attract and entertain young customers, who won prizes and candies when they collected a certain number of points. In an adult version of the game, the prizes came to include cigarettes and detergent. In America, the game boards remained basically horizontal, eventually developing into pinball games. In cramped Japan, however, some entrepreneur in the mid-1920s set a machine upright and added a spring-powered shooter and glass cover, and the Japanese game of pachinko was born. The name itself comes from the *pachi-pachi* sound made by the balls bouncing against the glass.

What is in a "Japanese PANCAKE"?

If someone invites you to eat this particular cuisine, do not expect the kind of dish that you might eat for breakfast. The Japanese "pancake" called *okonomiyaki* is usually made on a griddle built into the table and consists of a batter of simple flour and egg, to which one might add shrimp, squid, shredded cabbage, and pork. In some restaurants, the server may do the mixing and grilling, but in others the customer tends to those duties. Once the "pancake" is cooked on both sides, you can top it with your favorite combination of dried green seaweed, dried bonito flakes, Worcestershire sauce, mayonnaise, and/or chopped red ginger.

What are those pieces of PAPER stuck on temple pillars and ceilings?

These rectangular slips of paper called *senja-fuda*, literally "one thousand shrine card," carry the names of people, shops, or groups in large print, and the names of their towns of origin on top. Visitors stick them up as high as they can reach and leave them as proof of their pilgrimage, although many shrines and temples wish the visitors would take their memorials home with them.

What design is on the cover of Japanese PASSPORTS?

Passports in most nations bear the national seal. The United States, for instance, issues passports with an American eagle on the cover. Japan, however, has no national seal, and the Foreign Ministry has "borrowed"

the chrysanthemum seal of the imperial house. Why
it is the imperial seal rather than a cherry blossom,
for instance, is open to interpretation.

Why do a few public PHONES have two receivers?

These unusual phones allow for conversations among
three people. They are particularly popular with young
women who want to converse three ways easily. When
the phones were introduced in the summer of 1986,
the phone company was delighted to find that users
tended to talk 20% to 30% longer than on ordinary
single-handset phones. Despite this fact, however,
the dual-receiver phones never quite caught on, and
as they succumb to age, they are replaced with ordinary one-receiver phones. Thus, only a handful re-
main these days.

What is the difference among red, green, and gold public PHONES?

Long ago, when telephone rates were still a bargain
and red phones were ubiquitous, a ¥10 coin would
enable you to make a three-minute local call. Apart
from local calls, you could call anywhere in Japan
from Sapporo in the north to Kagoshima in the south,
as long as you had an ample supply of ¥10 coins—the
only type of payment the red public phones would
accept. According to NTT, the red phones are on the
way out and being steadily replaced by light green
phones which accept both coins and telephone cards.
A green phone with a gold plate or band can also be
used for overseas calls. Gray phones have jacks for
modem and fax connection, too. In stores and coffee
shops, you may find pink phones which are semi-
public, in that the owners of the establishments pay

the bills from the money deposited into the phones. Finally, in certain areas of Tokyo, there are gold phones. These are special, commemorative public phones installed in areas along the parade route of the wedding procession of the Crown Prince and Princess in 1993. Who says Japan does not have variety?

Why shouldn't one put one's PILLOW to the north?

As early as the Kofun and Yayoi periods, the traditional form of interment was such that the body was placed with the head to the north. This custom has continued to the present day, and the death connotation has made it taboo to sleep with one's head toward the north.

Why do Japanese call the sex industry the "PINK" industry?

The use of the color pink to describe the sex industry in general began with the movie business. The creator of the term "pink film" was a newspaper reporter who dealt primarily with the cinema. In describing certain types of films, he took the term *momo-iro yūgi*, or "love affair," and combined *momo-iro*, which by itself means "pink," with the word *eiga*, or "movie." The term "pink movie" hence entered the vocabulary in 1963, and has since been used to describe those movies that may contain sexually stimulating material but can still pass the movie codes and be shown in ordinary theaters.

What is the meaning of four bamboo POLES tied together with straw rope in an open lot?

Part of the religious ceremonies and rites observed in building houses and buildings even today, this square arrangement is the site of a purification rite conducted by a Shinto priest and attended by builder and owner to beseech the gods for divine protection over the safe construction of the structure. Once the ceremony is over, the bamboo, straw rope, and zigzag paper are left standing for a period.

Why does PORK cutlet always come with shredded cabbage?

When pork cutlet, or *ton-katsu*, was introduced around the turn of the century, there arose the problem of what vegetable to serve with it. Hot, cooked vegetables were troublesome since when help was short because of the Russo-Japanese War. The first candidate was chopped Chinese cabbage, but because it was not available year round, and became soggy even when it was, it found little favor with cooks. By trial and error, they then found that cabbage worked well.

How did the 〒 symbol come to represent POSTAL services?

The Japanese Ministry of Communications was established in 1871. In Japanese, the ministry's name was Teishin-sho, and it decided to use "T," the first letter of the romanized word, as the symbol for its mailboxes and postal codes. However, the ministry soon discovered that the letter "T" was used by other nations to indicate "insufficient postage," and so they decided to use the katakana letter *te*, for Teishin-sho.

Why are Buddhist PRIESTS in Japan allowed to marry?

Japanese Buddhism has traditionally had two types of priests. Lay priests did not renounce the world, but stayed with their families and took responsibilities for Buddhist services among the common people. Other priests, supported by the ruling class, devoted themselves to study and the performance of Buddhist services for the elite. Bound to celibacy, they were not formally allowed to have wives, although some took "hidden wives." In 1872, all priests were formally permitted to take wives, and at present marrying and remaining single are equally acceptable.

How do some Japanese try to keep RAIN away?

A piece of white paper or cloth is quickly turned into a *teruteru-bōzu* with a ball or a piece of stuffing and a string to tie it off at the neck. This makeshift doll is then hung from the eaves of the house, or even in a window, on the evening before an outing in the hope that no rain will come to spoil the event. This custom began in the Edo era, and these simple dolls are still made all around Japan by children who hope that the dolls will make their wishes come true. Given the length of the summer rainy season, not a few foreigners have been known to craft their own, too.

TERUTERU-BOZU

How much do Japanese READ?

Compared with the situation at the beginning of the Meiji era, when fewer than half its people could read, Japan has made tremendous strides in the field of literacy. Modern Japan can boast an almost universal literacy rate thanks to the positive effects of compulsory education and a booming publishing industry, although there is a trend away from books and the printed word in general. The Ministry of Education found in a survey in 1992, for example, that of all public high school students 21.2% tried to read books, but gave up halfway through for reasons ranging from boredom, to simple lack of ability to read or understand the contents of books. More astounding was the 38.4% who replied that they did not even want to read. So what about the booming publishing industry? What is being bought in large quantities is "how-to" books, computer-related materials, and *manga*.

Who wears RED on their birthdays?

It has been the custom for people who reach their sixtieth birthday to wear a red vest or other clothing to celebrate the occasion. Achieving sixty years was once quite an accomplishment, but many sixty-year-olds nowadays prefer to forego the celebration.

What has a RED face, a long nose, and glittering eyes?

Although you may recognize these qualities in an inebriated friend, in Japan the description is that of a *tengu*, a being from vernacular folklore which has the beak and wings of a bird, and the body and limbs of a human. Often portrayed as holding a feather fan and living in the top of a tall tree, the *tengu* is feared for his

TENGU

ability to possess and kidnap human beings. He is not completely malevolent, though. His magical powers can also be called on as a protection against evil, and he is believed to protect particular mountains, as well.

What does the combination of RED and white symbolize?

In addition to being the colors of the *hi-no-maru* flag, these colors are for felicitous occasions. Envelopes with red and white twisted paper strings are presented at wedding receptions. Long cloths with vertical red and white stripes are used at auspicious events to cover walls or to create enclosures. Red and white circular decorations made of artificial flowers are sent by businesses to celebrate openings of new shops or restaurants. Pachinko parlors imitate this custom with gaudy, imitation floral decorations of their own, but they tuck them into protective plastic wrapping and keep them out for months on end.

On a related note, similar decorations in black and white are for inauspicious occasions, such as wakes or funerals.

Do Japanese believe in RELIGIOUS teachings?

It is helpful to look at a 1994 *Yomiuri Shinbun* public opinion survey for answers to this question. The survey reports replies from people in age groups ranging from their twenties to their seventies and beyond. The percentages of respondents who answered that they believe in religious teachings ranged from 12% for people in their twenties, to 46% for those over seventy. When you put all the age groups together, 72% replied that they did not believe in religious teachings, while 26% said that they did.

Even among those who reported that they did not believe in religious teachings, however, 35% said that they believed in the existence of gods and/or buddhas, and 29% said that they believed that a person's soul remains after death.

Such replies strongly contrast with certain religious organizations' claims of memberships comprising significant portions of Japan's population.

How often do Japanese engage in RELIGIOUS practices?

A *Yomiuri Shinbun* survey queried people concerning three practices. First, it investigated whether they prayed before household shrines and/or Buddhist altars in their homes. Positive answers rose gradually from approximately 30% for respondents in their twenties, to over 60% for respondents over seventy. Next, the survey asked whether people visited their family graves at least once a year. People in their twenties replied in the affirmative more than 60% of the time, a percentage that rose gradually in proportion to the age group of respondents until it peaked at about 75% in the highest age group.

Answers to the first two questions suggested that there was an increase in actual religious "practice" as people grew older. A third question, though, revealed a trend toward the reverse. When asked whether they went to visit temples and shrines on the first day of each new year, close to 70% of those in their twenties replied that they did, whereas only 50% of those over seventy replied thus.

Obviously, the answers to questions concerning Japanese belief and practice depend on which questions you ask.

Why do RIGHT-WING groups use sound trucks?

The sturdily built sound truck, which can serve as a platform for political haranguing, a shelter from attack, and a broadcast booth for nationalistic music and speeches, is a favorite piece of equipment of right-wing groups because of its distinctive militaristic exterior and ability to make their views heard. The trucks and their high-volume broadcast power appear to be a means of compensating for a lack of presence in conventional political organs, such as the Diet.

Why shouldn't Japanese children play alone by the sides of RIVERS?

Japanese folklore tells of amphibious, green, supernatural creatures that dwell near water holes and whose great strength comes from water held in saucer-like receptacles on their heads. They are reputed to abduct and gruesomely murder small children whom they find playing alone by the riverside.

The *kappa* is said to be particularly fond of cucumbers, a fact which gives *kappamaki*, a vegetarian sushi

KAPPA

made with cucumber wrapped in rice and seaweed, its name.

Why do Japanese tie ROPES around big trees?

Thick straw ropes are often tied around particularly large, old trees in recognition of the special qualities that have enabled them to reach such size and longevity.

Why do Japanese hang giant ROPES at Shinto shrines?

Made by twisting strands of rice straw together, these ropes known as *shime-nawa* are used to designate sacred sites; they are also believed to have the power to fend off evil and illness. In a shrine, they may be hung before the main worship hall and the altar and across the entrance gate. They are also found placed around very old trees or rocks. At New Year's one finds them over doorways and even on car bumpers. The grandfather of all sacred ropes is the one at Izumo Shrine in Shimane Prefecture. It is 4 meters in circumference and weighs 1,500 kilograms.

How many rocks are there in the RYOANJI garden? What are they supposed to symbolize?

Although written with the characters for "Peaceful Dragon," the temple is actually anything but peaceful when the tourist buses pour through. Early in the morning, however, you will have an opportunity to count the stones and contemplate their meaning in relative silence. There are fifteen stones, although only fourteen can be seen at any one time. They are in groups of five, two, three, two, and three. They are islands, mountaintops, tigers, dragons in the sky, temples, and whatever else you might care to imagine them to be. To date, no one has ever proven that the original arranger of the stones meant any or all of these potential meanings. So, don't worry about "meaning"—just enjoy the garden.

How does one tell the difference between tokkyū, ikkyū, and nikyū ranks of SAKÉ

Have you ever felt socially inferior because you could not distinguish among the "special," "first," and "second" classes of Japan's national alcoholic beverage? Rest assured, you are not alone. And for good reason.

The grades of saké are fairly reliable when it comes to distinguishing among and comparing the products of a single manufacturer. A problem arises, however, when you compare different brewers' products.

What is labeled second class, or *nikyū*, may be a very nice drink indeed. Tax on a bottle of "special class," or *tokkyū*, is double that which is levied on first class, or *ikkyū*, which in turn is approximately twice that on *nikyū*. Each year, makers can submit samples of the products they wish to have tested for a certain class. If a maker decides not to submit a sample at all, its saké is automatically classified as the lowest-taxed *nikyū*. Many of the smaller, local brewers simply do not submit their products for testing. Thus, brewers who do submit their drinks for rating can be compared, either against themselves, or against other rated brewers with a degree of accuracy. Among the brewers who do not participate in this system, though, anything goes. There are some superb local brews that are "second class" only in terms of the taxation applied. Therefore, it is worth being adventuresome with the less expensive categories of saké. You may find a brew that is as inexpensive as it is delicious.

Why do Japanese drink SAKÉ from small cups?

In cultures where large animals were eaten, animal horns were among the first vessels used for making containers. When pottery and other materials came into use for liquids, the shape of the new cups generally remained narrow and deep. Lacking such large animals, but surrounded with marine life, the ancient Japanese are said to have taken seashells as their first vessels. With very little adaptation, these shells could be used for drinking liquids, and larger shells could

SAKÉ

be used as dishes for food. When pottery came into production, it followed the pattern of the shallow shell, giving birth to the custom of drinking saké from little cups.

What is a "SALARYMAN"?

When a Japanese friend describes himself as a *sarari-iman*, he is probably not aware that the term is not familiar to English-speakers. Actually, all he is saying is that he is a white-collar, or office, worker. White-collar workers tend not to identify themselves by occupation, but by the far broader category of "company employee" or "salaryman." To find out exactly what a person does requires further inquiry.

Why do Japanese sometimes put piles of SALT at entrances to eating and drinking shops?

This custom has its origin in ancient China. According to legend, an emperor had many beautiful mistresses whom he visited at night by oxcart. One smart lady asked the keeper of the Emperor's oxen to deprive them of salt for a few days. She then set out a pile of salt at her gate. As one might expect, the oxcart carrying the Emperor came to a halt in front of her gate, and she became a favorite with him. Nowadays, these piles, called *mori-jio*, are placed on both sides of the front doors of restaurants and drinking establishments as a means of inviting large numbers of customers to enter.

Who was SAN JORDI, and what did he have to do with books and roses?

According to Catalonian legend, San Jordi was a heroic knight who rescued a princess from an evil dragon.

As the dragon expired, its blood sprouted into a beautiful garden of red roses. As a token of his love, San Jordi made a garland out of the flowers and gave it to the princess.

So where do the books come in? They have nothing to do with San Jordi; but April 23, the date when San Jordi's Day is celebrated, is the anniversary of the deaths of William Shakespeare and Miguel de Cervantes Saavedra (*Don Quixote*). Thus, in Japan, it has become an occasion not only to give roses, but books, too.

Why is SASHIMI *served with fine strips of white radish?*

The white strips of radish serve as a background to enhance the aesthetic appeal of the fish so that one can "feast" with the eyes. In addition, the pleasant bitterness of the white radish, or daikon, also serves to refresh the tongue between bites of fish. Daikon strips are called *tsuma* in the Kanto region and *ken* in Kansai.

Where do Japanese SAVE *their money?*

Given that such a large portion of the populace considers itself "middle-class," it may come as a surprise that in 1993 the average household had savings of ¥13 million per household. This is the result of Japan's having an unusually high savings rate: approximately 14% of all income is hoarded away. Not even the burst of the bubble affected the average household's savings, because it seems that most individuals are conservative about the money they put away: 50.2% of money saved went into postal and bank accounts, while a mere 9.5% was invested in stocks.

Why do shops selling tea also usually sell dried SEA-WEED?

Although the two products are not consistently produced by the same regions, it has been customary since the late Edo period for shops selling green tea to deal also in *nori*, the lustrous laver that is used in sushi and other Japanese meals. The reason for this combination is that both require similar special handling to prevent damage due to moisture and to protect their important aromas.

What kind of SECONDHAND clothing in Japan can you definitely not get from the Salvation Army?

In 1985, an enterprising Japanese businessman identified a need yet to be satisfied by Japan's ever-lively sex trade. He opened a shop that bought used panties (complete with stains and smells) and school "sailor" uniforms from high school girls and sold them to customers with fetishes for these items. Since then, the *buru-sera* (from *burūmā*, or "bloomers," and *sera* for *sērā-fuku*, or "sailor uniform") industry has experienced a surprising boom in Japan. Typically, girls will buy panties for ¥100, and sell them to a *buru-sera* store for ten times that amount. The store will then pass them on to consumers for a price in the neighborhood of ¥3,000. Large numbers of otherwise unremarkable girls have managed to pick up quite a bit of spending money this way. More recently, even vending machines have been brought into this unique used clothing business.

Who is more willing to have SEX if there is mutual affection: Japanese or American youth?

The Management and Coordination Agency reported

in December 1993 on the views of Japanese people between the ages of eighteen and twenty-four regarding this topic. Asked whether they would be willing to have sex if there were mutual affection, 70.8% of people surveyed responded yes (compared with 51.3% for U.S. youth and 73.2% for French youth). Those who responded that sex should be avoided before marriage accounted for 5.3% of all replies (compared to 14% for U.S. youth and 1.7% for French youth). And you always thought that Japanese were prudish?

What are a "SHARP" pencil, a "klaxon," and a "Hotch-kiss"?

Shāpu, the Japanese word for mechanical pencil, was taken from the name of the American company which produced it, Eversharp.

Similarly, kurakushon, the Japanese word for an automobile horn, comes from the early manufacturer Klaxon. Hotchikisu, the Japanese word for stapler, is from the name of its American inventor, B. B. Hotch-kiss.

Why do you occasionally find a pair of SHOES carefully arranged in the middle of a parking lot?

Japanese drivers, particularly younger people, treat the insides of their cars like their homes. Accordingly, after entering the car, a driver changes from "outside" shoes into sandals for the duration of the drive. This practice also makes for easier driving. Unfortunately, some drivers get distracted in the process and drive away, leaving their shoes behind.

Why are SHRINE buildings and gates painted red?

The cinnabar red used for these Shinto structures has

the multiple functions of attracting attention at a distance, marking off the buildings as being sacred, and clearly setting them apart from ordinary buildings, very few of which are painted this color. In addition, it has been thought that cinnabar red has the power to ward off evil spirits.

Why do Japanese clap their hands at SHRINES?

Worshippers clap their hands at Shinto rituals to get the attention of the gods, a custom that makes it easy for non-Japanese to differentiate between shrines and a Buddhist temples. If a worshipper stands silently in front of the main building and places his palms together in prayer, as called for by Indian custom, then you are in front of a Buddhist temple.

Why do visitors put money in boxes at the front of SHRINES and temples?

The Japanese word for this money, *saisen*, is written with the characters for "temple visit" and "coin." It is offered during worship, sometimes in gratitude for the fulfillment of a previously made petition or prayer. The custom predates the Edo period, and even in ancient times it was the custom to offer newly minted coins to deities.

At New Year's, the boxes in front of Meiji Shrine and the Sensoji Temple at Asakusa are unable to handle the volume of incoming coins. When this happens, the temples erect larger frameworks, enabling worshippers to fling their coins from a distance.

Why are there usually water spigots and troughs in front of SHRINES?

Shinto is a religion of purification, and the washing

PORTABLE SHRINE

place, or *chōzuya*, just outside the inner gate is where worshippers purify themselves before going inside to pray. They take water in the ladles sitting by the trough to wash first the left hand, then the right hand, and finally to rinse the mouth. A similar rinsing of the mouth takes place in sumo during the preparations for a bout.

Why are some SHRINES portable?

The purpose of most Japanese festivals is to invite the deities to descend from heaven so that people can pray with them for good fortune, a good harvest, or for assistance in escaping danger. A ceremony within a shrine or other sacred place welcomes the gods to Earth. Local residents, usually men, then carry the portable shrine, which conveys the deity, around the local community and back to the shrine. There another ceremony is held to respectfully send the deity back to heaven.

Why do Japanese shake a rope attached to a bell at SHRINES?

In front of a shrine, there is a box for offerings, and hanging over it is a long rope attached to a large bell.

Worshippers usually shake the rope to "ring" the bell (which actually lacks a clapper) several times, then bow toward the shrine, clap their hands twice, and bow once more at the end of their prayers. The bell is believed to deliver the person's wishes to the deity of the shrine.

Why do Japanese restaurants have SIGNS that say ō-iri?

The characters mean "big" and "enter," which reflects the proprietors' hopes that droves of customers will do just that.

What is the cheapest place in Tokyo to SLEEP?

Virtually every major city in Japan has "capsule hotels" near its major train stations. Consisting of pre-fabricated sleeping compartments stacked one on top of another, these hotels offer bare minimum accommodations for late workers and last-train-miss-ers. Each horizontal unit contains a bed, reading light, radio and/or TV, a small shelf, and, of course, a shutter providing privacy. The facilities include a common toilet and showers. Though not intended for extended stays, these hotels do provide a place for a decent night's sleep for around ¥4,000.

Why do Japanese change SLIPPERS when entering the toilet?

This habit comes from the separation of the "clean" majority of the house from the "dirty" room where the facilities are located. Whether this is really necessary when the entire house is clean does not seem to enter into the matter. As you may realize, this custom is directly connected with that of removing one's shoes before entering a house, leaving the "dirty" outdoors outside when entering the clean "inside" of a home.

Are you intelligent if you are "SMART"?

This "borrowed" word is used among Japanese for its less frequently used meaning of "slim" or "stylish," rather than "intelligent." Either way, you can accept it as a compliment.

How did houses of prostitution come to be known as "SOAPLANDS"?

For decades these omnipresent establishments were known as *toruko-buro*, or "Turkish bath." The cause for the change was a Turkish diplomat's letters to Japanese newspapers during the months prior to a revision of the Law on Business Affecting Public Morals in 1985. To decide upon a less controversial euphemism, the Japan Bath Association held a competition to choose a new name. The winning entry was "soapland." It followed as a matter of course that the women who performed various services became known as "soap ladies."

Why does every child in Japan seem to know the same SONGS?

The Ministry of Education *Course of Study* stipulates that every school child in each respective grade should practice certain songs during the school year. With virtually uniform education nationwide through the nine years of compulsory education, children all over the country end up learning the same songs.

Where does the name SONY come from?

Sony's original name when it was founded in 1946

was the rather drab Tokyo Tsushin Kogyo, or "Tokyo Communications Industries." As time went on, however, company leaders Ibuka Masaru and Morita Akio decided that their organization needed a more exciting name. Both men liked the Latin word *sonus*, or "sound," and the warmth of the English words "sonny" and "sunny." They might have chosen "sonny" if they'd only needed to be concerned about its English meaning, but in Japanese the word could be read as *son-ne*, meaning something like "loss in value." They finally solved their problem by simply dropping one "n" from "sonny" and coining a name which had absolutely no connotations in Japanese, while at least sounding English in derivation.

Why do Japanese bring home from trips so many SOUVENIRS for other people?

The Japanese word *o-miyage*, which now means "souvenir," and is written with characters roughly meaning "product of the (local) land," traditionally referred to the amulets and talismans brought home from pilgrimages to shrines, a tradition beginning around the fifteenth century. When a member of a village was chosen to make a pilgrimage to the Ise Grand Shrine, for example, he could expect to receive *senbetsu*, or send-off money, from his friends. It was understood that for each contributor, he would return with some kind of religious artifact, food, or handicraft from the far-off region he visited. This tradition has been adapted to the modern day so that virtually any trip to a foreign country, or even a distant domestic location, will result in the traveller's bringing back a load of small gifts for friends, relatives, and colleagues, even though they probably have not provided any send-off money. So although the word "souvenir" often implies something that one brings home for oneself, an *o-miyage* is something that one gets for others.

Where does the money from SPEEDING TICKETS go?

The money that you have to pony up when the law comes down on you for speeding goes to no less august an institution than the Bank of Japan. It is held there until its semiannual distribution to the local governments most in need of new sidewalks, traffic signals, and road signs. Although law enforcement people do not officially acknowledge it, there does appear to be a quota for traffic violations, including speeding, that police are expected to issue. At least it all goes to a good cause.

What is the most popular SPORT in Japanese high schools?

Given the national preoccupation with the spring and summer high school invitational baseball tournaments, you could not be faulted for assuming that the answer to this question can be found on a diamond. Actually, though, baseball is only number four among high schoolers. The three most popular sports among high school students, from most to less, are basketball, volleyball, and soccer.

Why do cigarette shops sell STAMPS?

If you search the area near your local mailbox, you will usually find a store with a sign announcing that it's selling postage stamps, postcards, domestic-use aerogrammes called "mini-letters," and revenue stamps. It will likely be at a shop selling cigarettes.

No special training is required for this business, nor must the seller be a cigarette vendor. Anyone within 50 meters of the mailbox can apply to the Post Office to be appointed to sell stamps. But why would anyone apply? Is there money to be made from taking the trouble?

The postal service pays the shop 10% on sales up to and including ¥100,000, but the rate declines as sales totals rise, sinking to 0.5% on sales totaling ¥1,500,002 and over. So, why go to the trouble of selling an ¥80 stamp, when it will only bring in ¥8, and customers will be few and far between? The answer is that the shop also sells revenue stamps necessary for legal documents such as contracts and visa applications at ¥5,000, ¥10,000, and ¥20,000 a pop, and it receives the same percentages on these stamps as it does on the postage ones. If the shop is conveniently located near a government office or in a business district, sales can rise quickly.

What are those animal-like STATUES in front of Shinto shrines?

Called *koma-inu*, or Korean dogs, these animals are highly stylized lions. You will notice that one has its mouth open and the other has its mouth closed. The former is pronouncing the syllable *a*, and the latter is

KOMA-INU

is pronouncing *un*. These sounds were originally the first and last ones of the Sanskrit alphabet and symbolize the beginning and the end of the universe.

Why do people who commit SUICIDE take their shoes off beforehand?

In both cinema and the real world, a person determined to end it all will often leave his or her shoes neatly arranged on the beach facing the ocean, or on the ledge at the top of the building from which he or she intends to depart. This practice derives from the belief that dying with bare feet enables a person to leave the dirt of this world behind before entering the next world.

What does the winner of a major SUMO tournament get?

He becomes the proud recipient of a car, a year's supply of gasoline, one thousand *shiitake* mushrooms, one cow's weight of beef, and a year's supply of cola.

Why do SUMO wrestlers throw salt into the ring before a bout?

Contestants show their determination to fight by purifying themselves before their bout. This ritual includes rinsing their mouths with water and wiping their bodies with paper. They then reach into the basket of salt at their corner of the ring to take a handful with which to purify the ring before they enter it. This purification of body, mind, and ring is said to have been part of tradition since Edo days.

Why are SUMO wrestlers so fat?

Many of the boys who enter the sumo world are

recruited because of their physical endowments (large bone structure, ability to gain weight, etc.), but not all aspirants to the world of sumo start out as heavyweights. To be accepted as a trainee in any of the stables that falls under the jurisdiction of the Japan Sumo Association, one has to weigh a minimum of 75 kilograms and measure a minimum of 1.73 meters in height. Once an aspiring wrestler is accepted into a stable, it becomes his duty to practice hard and gain weight. The main source of weight gain is the midday meal, generally the high-calorie stew called *chanko-nabe*, which contains a selection of meat, fish, and vegetables.

Today, top-ranking wrestlers average about 140 kilograms, almost double the required minimum for entrance; in earlier days, however, the average weight was lower. The recent appearance and success of lighter, more muscular wrestlers like Chiyonofuji, Takanohana, Terao, and Kyokudozan may herald a return to the relatively compact wrestlers of the past.

What do SUMO wrestlers do after they retire from competition?

They may become heads or coaches of stables, work as media commentators, or even open up their own restaurants specializing in *chanko-nabe*, the filling stew eaten by active wrestlers who are trying to gain weight.

How can you tell who wins a SUMO bout?

Although the preparation for an upper-division bout is limited to a period of four minutes, the bout itself may be over in a few seconds. Since both contestants may have ended up out of the ring or on the ground, you may be left wondering who actually won. The simple rule is that the first wrestler to touch the ground with any part of his body other than the bottom of his feet loses. The rules in this regard are so vigorously upheld that even if a wrestler's topknot touches—which has happened—the contestant loses. Because of these strict rules and the fierce competitiveness of the wrestlers, you will see very few attempts to cushion a fall with an outstretched arm. When both men tumble out of the ring, the first one who touches down loses, and when that fails as a determinant, there is a rule that the one who first lost all chance of recovering is the one who loses.

How much is in the envelopes given to winners of SUMO bouts?

At the beginning of a bout between popular and/or winning *sumō-tori*, the ring announcers circle the ring carrying banners that show the names of companies or other sponsors. Each banner represents ¥60,000 offered as *kenshōkin*, or "encouragement money," for the winner of the bout. After the bout is decided, the two wrestlers bow to one another, and the loser leaves the ring first. The winner makes chopping motions with his hand in the four cardinal directions in gratitude to the gods who have helped him to his victory. If there are envelopes to be taken from the referee's paddle, the wrestler then takes what is being offered him and leaves the ring. The winner does not "take all" in this case, because for each ¥60,000 at stake in the match the envelope contains only ¥30,000. The Sumo Association keeps ¥5,000 for printing the sponsor's name on the day's program and announcing it over the loudspeaker, and the other ¥25,000 is set aside for the eventual settlement with the tax man.

What happens if a SUMO-TORI'S belt comes off during a bout?

Since the wrestler's belt, or *mawashi*, is some 9 meters long and made of silk, the chances of its coming off are minimal. If the belt is obviously coming loose, the referee is also close at hand to momentarily halt the bout and retie the belt. Despite these precautions, belts have come off several times in this century, much to the embarrassment of everyone concerned. Some wrestlers still purposely tie their belts loosely to make it difficult for their opponents to get solid grips, but Sumo Association rules stipulate that a wrestler whose belt actually comes off automatically loses.

Why do so many SUMO-TORI names have the words yama and umi in them?

Sumo has always many included many aspects of traditional culture in its rituals. In early days, wrestlers represented the gods of their respective regions. The regions from which wrestlers hailed were announced before each bout, along with their names. The wrestlers were often given the names of local mountains (*yama*) or lakes (*umi*) because they were felt to be reenacting a legendary bout between Yamasachihiko, the mountain god, and Umisachihiko, the god of lakes and seas.

Why are SUSHI makers all men?

There are at least two explanations for this fact. One is that the temperature of men's hands is lower than that of women's and therefore the fish is not unnecessarily warmed during preparation. A second theory is that a taboo related to menstruation prevents women from preparing sushi. Whatever the actual reason, it is extremely rare for a woman to actually cut and prepare the fish, even if she may assist with the preparation of rice and other ingredients behind the scenes.

Why are nigiri served two at a time at SUSHI shops?

Many people think that a pair of *nigiri* is just right for savoring the taste of the fish. Also, when the customer is seated at and ordering at the counter in front of the sushi maker, the serving of two *nigiri* helps the sushi maker get the timing right so that the food is always prepared just before the customer eats it, eliminating the wait.

What are the Japanese SYMBOLS for "yes" and "no"?

When a Japanese makes a list of people invited to a party and then marks the names of those who accept the invitation, he or she will mark the names of the attendees with a *maru* (O) and those of the the absentees with a *batsu* (X). Similarly, the *maru* is also used to mark things that are correct or "okay," while the *batsu* mark is used for mistakes or things that are missing. This is why some Japanese are thrown off when confronted with a list on which things are checked with the good, old Western "check" mark (✓).

Why do Japanese hang wooden TABLETS in front of shrines and temples?

Prayer tablets called *e-ma* are sold to visitors who wish to write upon them wishes for success in such endeavors as entrance exams, locating marriage partners, and delivery of children. The characters for *e-ma* mean "picture" and "horse," and the word comes from

E-MA

the days when horses (both flesh or wooden) were presented as offerings to shrines. The tablets once primarily had paintings of horses on them, but now depict many other figures too, including the animals of the Chinese zodiac, or depictions of the respective temples or shrines at which they're being sold.

How much TALLER have Japanese grown since 1945?

The average height of twenty-year-old males has increased by 6.5 centimeters to 171.5 centimeters as of 1992. The average female of the same age has grown by 5 centimeters to 158.3 centimeters.

Are all TATAMI mats created equal?

The traditional way of measuring the size of the rooms of a Japanese house is by how many mats (90 centimeters by 180 centimeters) the floor has. This used to be a fine standard, because everyone knew how big a mat was, and could picture the space of a four-and-a-half or six-mat room. But when the urban population exploded, and construction of new houses and condominiums boomed, the size of mats shrank accordingly. So do not be fooled. A six-mat room in a city apartment building does not just seem smaller than a six-mat room in a house in the suburbs—it really is.

How much does a full-body TATTOO cost?

The tattooist sets to work only after careful planning of the design and thorough consultation with the person who is to become the canvas. Each session lasts approximately one hour and costs in the neighborhood of ¥10,000; the client has one session every few days for between two and three years. Since a complete tattoo requires several hundred hours, it is painful not only physically, but economically, as well. When all is said and done, a full body tattoo costs ¥3 million and up.

Why do yakuza have TATTOOS?

In Japan, tattooing as a form of punishment was frequently carried out until the early eighteenth century, especially for robbers. Despite these earlier negative associations of tattooing, however, having oneself tattooed became a kind of fashion in Osaka and Edo during the early nineteenth century among artisans, construction workers, firemen, and denizens of the Yoshiwara red-light district. Sensitive to the views of the "enlightened" Westerners who visited Japan, the Meiji government attempted to ban the custom, but never succeeded in suppressing it entirely.

In this century, the tattoo has been taken over by gangsters who choose to endure the sting of the needle in order to show their identity, resolve, ability to tolerate pain, and devotion to the path they've chosen. Currently there is no requirement that one have a tattoo in order to become a gangster, and in fact some gangs actually forbid the practice, but the mystique continues. And, of course, the mere sight of a tattoo strikes fear into the hearts of ordinary citizens, a fact that obviously works to the advantage of the gangsters.

What are TENUGUI for?

Whether it a person be a construction worker, a noodle vendor, or even a homemaker picking up around the house, he or she is as likely as not to have a piece of cotton cloth wrapped, tied, or draped around the head to mop up sweat and repel dust. Nowadays distributed as advertisements of sightseeing spots, *tenugui* are also still used by kabuki actors to indicate they are playing certain types of roles. They are also used by the people who carry portable shrines at festivals to indicate their affiliation with a sponsoring group, a professional association, or even a company. Even hikers use them for a very simple task—to wipe away perspiration.

Why is there no TIPPING in Japan?

Apparently, Japan has never observed the custom of tipping in restaurants, taxis, or hotels. Servers, drivers, and bellhops were full-time employees and they were paid regular wages. Customer satisfaction was reflected in the success of their employers, and employees benefited in that they continued to have jobs. Despite the fact that part-timers now increasingly fill these jobs, the custom of not tipping remains, so one need not be troubled by having to pay gratuities on top of the already-high fees.

Why do Japanese stick needles in TOFU?

Back in the days when more people used needles to sew kimono and other clothing, almost every household set aside one day a year to express their gratitude to their indispensable needles and also take a day off from sewing. By sticking well-worn needles that have broken or bent in soft material like tofu, seamstresses and kimono makers show their appreciation, and even affection, for them by giving them a final, soft material in which to rest. This tradition is still observed on February 8 every year.

Which direction does one face when using a Japanese-style TOILET?

Squat facing the direction with the hood to successfully relieve yourself in a Japanese-style pot. If you are less than impressed by the cleanliness of Japanese-style toilets in stations and other public places, you might find comfort in the fact that the situation was even worse at the turn of the century, when even women stood to urinate.

What kind of TOILETS did the Heian nobles employ?

Whereas most Heian people completed their duties in the great outdoors, it would have been very difficult for a finely dressed court lady or lord to follow the same pattern. They managed quite well with a simple portable toilet consisting of no more than a box. A designated servant brought in the box and, once business was taken care of, removed and cleaned it.

What is a TOKO-NO-MA?

This alcove, which is raised several inches above the tatami floor of a Japanese-style room, first appeared in the Muromachi period. An easy way to visualize it might be to think of it as looking somewhat like a wide, shallow closet without doors. It originated as a place for hanging a scroll with a Buddhist motif, under which was placed a small table with an incense burner. The contemporary alcove, when people even bother to include it as a part of their homes, may display calligraphy or a decorative scroll, and below it may be a vase of flowers or some artwork.

Which is taller: TOKYO TOWER or the Eiffel Tower?

The Eiffel Tower, built for the Paris Exposition of 1889, measures 300 meters, while Tokyo Tower measures 333 meters. Built in 1958, Tokyo Tower supports an antenna that broadcasts television, FM, and public information channels.

When was TOOTH BLACKENING practiced?

Through the Heian period, the blackening of teeth was primarily a sign of a court lady's having attained womanhood. In subsequent centuries, the custom spread beyond the palace and came to be practiced by men of the nobility and the samurai class. Falling out of fashion among males in the latter half of the Edo era, the tradition continued to be observed widely by women at various levels of society. It finally died out, once and for all, at the beginning of this century.

Want to revive the custom yourself? The blackening mixture can be made by oxidizing nails or other bits of iron in a variety of liquids.

What was the purpose of the TOPKNOT and who used to wear them?

Among the many elements of mainland Asian culture that Japan adopted between the fifth and eighth centuries was the wearing of topknots. As the hierarchy of society grew more complex, each rank came to have its own particular hairstyle, including types of topknots. Among males, it became customary to have a topknot at the back of the head while keeping the front shaved. During the Edo period, the military rulers established detailed rules for each of the four classes of society regarding housing, clothing, and even hairstyles, including who could wear what type of topknot. So accustomed did males grow to the wearing of topknots that at the beginning of the Meiji era, when the government was eager to "catch up" with the West, it felt even compelled to call on the populace to surrender their topknots in order to appear more civilized to Americans and Europeans. Since that era, it is only *sumō-tori* and a few eccentrics who retain the custom of wearing a topknot.

Why do Japanese insist on calling green TRAFFIC lights "blue"?

When the first traffic signals were installed in Japan, they were red, yellow, and blue. After it was discovered that green lights were more visible at a distance than blue lights, the signals' blue lenses were gradually replaced with green ones. Even so, the original names have remained to the present day. So when Japanese insist that the light is blue, it is because they have learned to call it that, not because Japan's color scheme is unique, or Japanese and non-Japanese eyes see colors differently.

How can one tell the capacity of subway and Japan Rail TRAIN cars?

Each JR coach has its designated passenger capacity painted on its outside. The capacity includes not only the total number of seats, but also the number of straps for standing passengers on such trains as commuter trains. When the number of passengers goes beyond this designated number, it exceeds 100% of capacity. The most meaningful way to describe the crowding on the train is to note that at 200%, normal rush-hour crowding, it is impossible to open a newspaper. At 250%, people cannot even move. Past that, the problem reaches the point so that train attendants are required to engage in the notorious practice of physically stuffing passengers into the cars so that the doors can close.

Why don't Japanese eat on certain TRAINS?

Generally when seats on a train are lined up along the side of the car, the train is for commuting, and one rarely sees a Japanese take out a meal and dig in. Eating on such a train would be considered poor etiquette, because everyone along the opposite side could watch. This principle does not seem to change even when a commuter train travels several hours between an urban center and the countryside.

By contrast, when the seats face the front or rear of the train, and trays protrude from windows or fold out of the backs of seats airplane-style, like on the *shinkansen*, the situation changes. Since the number of people who can gawk is minimized, the box lunches and snacks come out readily.

Why do Japanese TRAINS stop around midnight?

According to public-relations officials, there are several reasons for stopping trains late at night. First, after a certain time, the numbers of passengers dwindles to the point where it becomes less profitable to run trains. Next, the maintenance work that is necessary to keep Japan's overtaxed trains running would be dangerous for railway workers if they had to venture into tunnels or onto tracks while the trains were going. Finally, if trains ran all night, it would spell financial trouble for the taxi industry, which earns a great portion of its income ferrying home people who have missed the last trains.

What do red TRIANGLES on the outsides of buildings mean?

These symbols on the outside of some windows and doors of buildings show firefighters where they can enter a building in case of emergency. It is the responsibility of the occupants to keep clear paths leading inside from those entrances. Building codes require buildings over three stories to have these marks if there are no outside stairways for access.

What is the trio of green lights on top of TRUCK cabs?

Traffic regulations require that a truck over five tons have a set of three green lights installed on the top of the cab and visible from the front of the truck. The light above the passenger's side automatically goes on when the truck starts to move. The light above the driver's seat goes on when the truck reaches 30 kph and the middle light goes on when the truck accelerates to 60 kph.

Why is raw TUNA rolled in rice and seaweed called tekka?

For those who had the color of hot iron in mind, we regret to note that *tekka*, literally "red-hot iron," has nothing to do with the production of metalware. The name originated in gambling dens called *tekka-ba*, where the game was dice. When the action was in full swing, no one wanted to leave or order food that would require eating with both hands. The ideal food could be eaten with one hand, leaving the other hand free for throwing the dice. Rather than eat a plebeian food like *kappamaki*, cucumber rolled in rice and seaweed, it became customary to consume the more elegant raw tuna rolled in rice and seaweed. The name of the sushi comes not from its ingredients, but from the place where it was often consumed.

Who uses a "TWO-SHOT *telephone club*"?

This new variety of business allows a man and a woman who do not know one another to hold a conversation on the telephone. Since the general motivation of such callers is to arrange a tryst, it came as quite a shock to the national organization of PTAs when they found that 17% of eighth- and ninth-grade girls had placed calls to such clubs.

Why do so many children ride UNICYCLES?

In the Ministry of Education's *Course of Study*, which went into effect in 1992, unicycle riding is one of the "suggested" physical education activities for students' third and fourth years at elementary schools. Although the schools may introduce the activity earlier or later, or not employ it at all, as of this writing over 90% of Japanese primary schools are teaching their students how to ride. In addition to the physical benefits of developing coordination and balance, the Japan Unicycle Association also asserts that unicycling's social aspects make it an appealing activity. It requires persistence and practice: even those with good coordination cannot immediately master the cycle. Conversely, even those who are not good at other sports or track and field events can master the cycle if they stick to it. For these reasons, the unicycle has been widely adopted.

Why do schoolchildren change their UNIFORMS on June 1 and October 1?

The custom of changing between heavier and lighter clothing originated in the Heian period, when there were more stages in the process. Today, the custom is seen not only in schools were uniforms are required, but also in department stores and offices where women wear uniforms. Unfortunately, the change of uniforms does not allow for hot days in spring or cool days in the rainy season in June.

Where did Japanese school UNIFORMS come from?

The model for the male uniform was the Japanese army's sergeant's combat uniform, which in turn came

SCHOOL UNIFORM

from European army uniforms. The first school uniform in the nation, it was adopted for use in 1885 at what today is Tokyo University. The reason for adopting the uniform was to make students obey the rules and to make it easy for them to act as a group. In addition, becoming an officer in the military was a goal of the elite, so students were happy to wear them. Uniforms for females were introduced in the Taisho era. Their tops were based on European sailor uniforms, and their skirts were designed to match.

Why are four and nine UNLUCKY?

The Japanese character for the number four is pronounced *shi*, the same sound as that of another character meaning "death." The Japanese character for the number nine is pronounced *ku*; a different character with the same pronunciation means "suffering." Because of the similarity in these sounds, these two numbers are considered unlucky. Therefore, when the examination rooms of a hospital are numbered, for instance, the room numbers will usually be 1, 2, 3, 5, and so on, avoiding the unlucky numbers.

Why do Japanese men and kids URINATE in the street?

In earlier decades, this custom was much more common. Men, particularly under when the influence of alcohol, seemed hardly to hesitate at all when the need arose. In recent times, the social climate has changed to make it less acceptable to relieve oneself at the nearest wall. Children, however, are exempt from this unwritten code, and it is not uncommon to see harried parents helping their children tend to a pressing need.

OBON OFFERINGS

Why do Japanese put animal dolls made of VEGETA-BLES and toothpicks in front of their gates in late summer?

In some areas, it is thought that the souls of departed ancestors will return to their ancestral homes riding horses and cows. To ensure that ancestors will arrive home unerringly, cow-shaped dolls made with egg-plants, and horse-shaped dolls made with cucumbers are set at the gate facing each house at the beginning of the Bon festival.

Why is "VEGETABLE SHOP" written with the characters for "eight-hundred-shop"?

Originally, shops selling vegetables were called *ao-ya*, literally "green grocers." Because they sold many other kinds of foodstuffs, too, including dried foods, seaweed, and nuts, they began to be called *yao-ya*, written with the characters for "eight hundred" and "shop." The number eight hundred in Japanese tradition denotes a very large number of items, which is exactly the message that the shopkeepers wanted to convey.

What can you buy from Japanese VENDING machines?

In addition to the standard drinks and snacks, you can buy fresh flowers, fresh eggs, condoms, beer, whiskey, comic books, magazines (pornographic and otherwise), underwear (new or used), stockings, and prepaid telephone cards. In a token effort to keep vending-machine alcohol out of the hands of minors, such vending machines are set so that they automatically shut down after 11 P.M.

Where would you find a "VIKING" in Japan?

Most likely, a "Viking" would be found in a hotel restaurant. For referring to buffets, the more cumbersome word "smorgasbord" seems to have been passed over in favor of the similarly Scandinavian-sounding "Viking."

Where can one find a "VIRGIN road"?

A virgin road can be found in a wedding chapel, of course. It is the central aisle, often covered with a special white carpet, upon which the bride treads on her way to the altar. Interestingly enough, some brides travel this road not on the arm of their fathers, but by themselves. Whether all of these brides are actually virgins, of course, is another matter altogether, as statistics elsewhere in this book will suggest.

How do Japanese families keep WARM during the winter?

Very few Japanese homes are equipped with central heating, and the main source of heating is portable heaters which burn kerosene. The typical Japanese household also owns a *kotatsu*, a short table with a heating unit and quilted cover, where one can sit and at least keep arms and legs warm. Traditionally, a one-story home had a recess under the table frame and a charcoal heater underneath. One could sit upright, as if in a chair, with legs dangling down into the recess. The modern adaptation of this is an electric heating unit in a lightweight table which can be moved anywhere in a room. One simply sits with legs hidden under the quilt, which traps the *kotatsu's* heat inside.

Why is WASABI *served with sashimi?*

First of all, this green, fiery-tasting horseradish tastes good with raw fish. Second, it helps to cut down on the fish's odor. Third, it has an anti-bacterial effect.

How much do elaborate WEDDING *receptions cost?*

A typical wedding includes a short ceremony in Shinto or Christian fashion, attended by relatives and very close friends, followed by a wedding reception to which as many as one hundred guests may be invited for a sit-down meal of magnificent dishes. The entertainment may include one or more of the following: the cutting of an enormous (and fake) wedding cake; several changes of clothes by the bride and groom;

KOTATSU

speeches; songs; the lighting of a candle on each of the guest tables; and the distribution of gifts for all the guests to take home with them.

An annual survey carried out by the Sanwa Bank Home Consultant section for 1994 pegs the cost of the average reception at ¥3.4 million. At the top-flight Imperial Hotel, the cost per guest is about ¥40,000, making a banquet for one hundred guests a princely ¥4 million! Who pays for these hotel receptions? Generally, the parents, who for all their private moaning about the cost, seem determined to give their children what they did not have when the economy was much gloomier.

Why are there so many WEDDING ceremonies on certain days and none on others?

The Japanese have long maintained a Chinese custom which divides the calendar into cycles of six days, called *rokki*. The names of the days in the cycle are *senkachi*, *tomo-biki*, *senmake*, *butsumetsu*, *taian*, and *shakkō*. The most auspicious day for the main events of life, such as starting a new business, beginning construction of a house, becoming engaged, and getting married, is *taian*, or "great peace," and the next best is *tomo-biki*, literally "pull a friend." When one of these days happens to fall on a Saturday or Sunday, when most people are off from work, the wedding halls run at full steam. When a Saturday or Sunday coincides with the most inauspicious day of the cycle, *butsumetsu*, or "Buddha's death," the same wedding halls have to offer special discounts to attract couples. On the other days of the cycle, certain parts of each day are auspicious, while other parts are inauspicious.

Where did "WHITE DAY" come from?

The Japanese imported the custom of celebrating St. Valentine's Day on February 14 and, with the encouragement of the chocolate makers, settled on chocolate as "the" gift to give. The catch is that, in the Japanese version of the holiday, females give gifts of chocolate to males. Then, unwilling to let a good thing alone, confectioners invented "White Day" (celebrated on March 14) to give the guys a chance to reciprocate. Not restricting themselves to chocolate, though, men have been a little more creative in their choices of return gifts to the ladies. A variety of white items, such as underwear—a gift choice that may go over better in the home than the workplace—are known to have been offered as White Day presents.

Why are some WOMEN especially careful when they reach the ages of nineteen and thirty-three?

The nineteenth and thirty-third years have long been considered unlucky for women, and although people are less superstitious nowadays, some women will still visit Shinto shrines during these years, known as *yakudoshi*, to be ritually purified or at least obtain amulets to prevent misfortune or ill health. For men, the corresponding unlucky years are twenty-five, forty-two, and sixty. Given the fact that these years are often turning points in their careers, they may also feel uneasy during these times, whether or not they pay heed to superstition.

Why is WRAPPING purchases and gifts so important to Japanese?

Whether a clerk in a store wrapping a purchase for a customer, or someone wrapping a gift for a friend, almost any Japanese will exercise considerable care to ensure that a present is appropriately "dressed" in a way that shows appreciation for its recipient. For example, it is not unusual for a store clerk to wrap an already-wrapped item in the wrapping paper of the store and then put it into a paper shopping bag. Although department stores are showing slightly more environmental consciousness by cutting down on wrapping, they are often afraid to cut back too much, for fear that customers will not feel sufficiently "appreciated."

On a formal occasion such as a wedding, a gift to a friend is always wrapped once, then covered with a sheet of white paper. It is then wrapped with paper strings called *mizuhiki*. One then writes on the paper not the recipient's name, but one's own, so that the recipient will know whom it is from. This is important because it is not customary to open presents in the presence of the giver.

Why do YAKUZA sometimes chop off their pinkies?

In earlier days, the *yakuza* weapon of choice was the Japanese sword. In order to hold this two-handed sword, the little finger of the wielder's left hand would have to grasp the bottom of the handle. To surrender this little finger, therefore, came to mean to give up a certain degree of physical capability and, by extension, influence.

Times change, and now certain doctors have a sideline replacing missing digits. Nonetheless, this agonizing ritual—performed without benefit of anesthesia or trained medical personnel—persists in Japan's demimonde, a potent deterrent to would-be deviants from the strict rules of the underworld.

What is a "YANKEE MAMA"?

Originally, the word "Yankee" was used to refer to high school girls still in school uniforms who would apply full make-up and try to pass themselves off as young adults. More recently, however, a new social phenomenon brought about a variation on this term. "Yankee mama" is the term used to refer to "Yankee" teenage mothers who go their own way in the raising of their children. Despite a natural desire for a happy home life on one hand, they are unable to adjust to settled existence and find it difficult to fit into local networks of housewives. They stand out because of their orange-dyed hair, excessive make-up, loud fashions, the copycat clothes into which they put their children, and their love of karaoke and late nights.

Why do Japanese buy decorative rakes at YEAR'S END?

People who buy these elaborately decorated *kuma-de* hope to "rake it in" during the coming year. The November fairs in Tokyo at various Otori shrines, which are dedicated to the gods of prosperity and happi-

KUMA-DE

ness, are held on the days of the cock, or *tori*. *Tori* here is a pun on a homophone that means "take in."

Is *a* "YELLOW CAB" *a taxi?*

"Yellow Cab" is a pejorative term for young Japanese women living or visiting abroad who are willing to make themselves "available" to local men with very little encouragement. The taxi metaphor comes about in that "yellow cabs" are said to be ready to pick up anyone: easy to get on, easy to get off. (The "yellow" part needs no explanation, perhaps.) This term—and phenomenon—achieved notoriety with the publication of journalist Ieda Shoko's controversial book *Yellow Cab* in 1991.

Why *do* Japanese *say* en *instead of* YEN?

The character for yen was originally pronounced *wen*, but over the course of the evolution of the Japanese language, all of its "w" sounds except *wa* disappeared. Consequently, during the Edo period, Japanese simply pronounced the word as they do today: *en*. Westerners at that time, however, tended to represent the Japanese *e* sound in romaji as "ye," so that *en* became "yen." Similarly, Edo was written as "Yedo," and even today, a premium beer named after Ebisu, the god of good fortune, is spelled "Yebisu" by its brewer, apparently to add a feeling of tradition to the packaging.

What is a "Y SHIRT"?

Business or dress shirts, regardless of their actual colors, are called "white shirts" in Japanese. When the Japanese rendition of white, *howaito*, is shortened to *wai*, it has the pronunciation of the English letter "Y," so the local word simply becomes "Y-shirt."

What are the ZIGZAG strips of white paper found at shrines?

These streamers appear in gold, silver, or several different colors, but the majority are white. These paper strips, or *gohei*, are attached to wands (also called *gohei*) that shrine priests or young female attendants wave during rituals to beckon to the gods or as a gesture of purification. They are also attached to the straw ropes that mark sacred precincts.